This is a politically incorrect book. In this era of research-based solutions and data-driven decision making, I offer instead personal observation and anecdotes. Over a year's time, I walked the halls of schools to see how technology was actually being used in classrooms. In this book, I share what I saw and heard, offer conclusions, and recommend ways that we can get our schools out of the technology fix they are in.

► ► ►

The Technology Fix

The Promise and Reality of Computers in Our Schools

Introduction ◂◂◂

MY FIRST COMPUTER WAS ONE OF THE ORIGINAL APPLES. THERE wasn't much software available when I bought it. "Try this," the dealer suggested, placing a box labeled "VisiCalc" on the counter. I took it home, loaded it, and was hooked. VisiCalc, the original spreadsheet program, gave me a sense of power I'd seldom felt. Subsequently improved upon by Lotus 1-2-3 and Microsoft Excel, VisiCalc is long forgotten, but the romance with computers that this software sparked in me remains.

That spark has turned into a steady flame over the past two decades, and the romance has turned into enduring love. Admittedly, I was somewhat fickle in my earlier days, adopting and discarding my Commodore, TRS-80, Osborne, KayPro, IBM Jr., Macintosh, and several PCs. My current *amour,* my Dell, is the one that I now consult upon waking. Through it, I get my news, communicate by instant messages with my sons in San Francisco and Boston, stay in touch with topics of interest on several mailing lists, do business through a constant stream of e-mail, buy my clothes, and listen to music.

Computers have also been essential to my professional life. In 1982, I developed math and reading programs for the TRS-80. Since then, I have guided the creation of educational software programs and Web sites for publishers, nonprofit organizations, and government agencies. Many of the programs I developed were state-of-the-art . . . on the cutting edge. Few endured past version 2.0.

Twenty-four months ago, the question "Why?" beat in my mind insistently. Why did these programs—so carefully thought out, creatively designed, expertly programmed, and favorably reviewed—have such negligible commercial value? My programs were not the only ones that stagnated in the market. Educational publishers across the United States have poured millions of dollars into software products. Several handfuls have been smashing successes. The vast majority have lost money.

Publisher investments in educational technology have been paltry compared with government investments. Since 1980, federal, state, and local governments invested tens of billions of dollars in hardware, software, teacher training, and support staff. Over the past couple of years, I have had a nagging sense that this investment wasn't paying off, but I could not put my finger on why. Part of my concern was surely rooted in disappointment at the meager sales of the products that I (and many others) developed. Furthermore, school performance as measured by the SAT and the National Assessment of Educational Progress has shown little improvement since computers were introduced into classrooms. Why, I asked, has this powerful tool, so essential to my own life, seemed to have had no measurable impact on school performance?

One evening, as the questions sloshed around in my mind, I picked up *The Tipping Point* by Malcolm Gladwell. In this *New York Times* best-seller, Gladwell identifies several factors that ignite social, medical, and technological wildfires. He examines the case of Hush Puppy shoes, a nearly extinct style of the 1960s that found sudden new life and startling success in the mid-1990s. He looks at causes for the drop in New York's crime rate, at the suddenness with which whole neighborhoods have fallen victim to white flight, at the speed of the AIDS epidemic, and at other sudden and widespread changes.

Gladwell's book got me thinking: What will be the tipping point for technology to thrive in the classroom? What conditions must exist for the technology investment to pay off? Is it simply a question of better teacher training, newer computers, more reliable networks, improved software, and broader access to the Internet? How will yesterday's promises translate into tomorrow's reality?

▸ ▸ ▸

Like many who found that computers transformed the way they worked, learned, and communicated, I believed the bold promises about the benefits of technology in the classroom:

• Student-centered classrooms, where computers tailor instruction to the individual needs of every learner would replace the teacher-centered classroom.

• Students would no longer be passive recipients of information. Technology would empower them to become active participants in the construction of their own knowledge. With access to the world's ever-expanding pool of knowledge, school children would pose relevant questions and find their own answers, often in concert with students in distant lands. They would communicate with renowned scientists, writers, historians, and public figures, joining to solve real-world problems. The barriers of the classroom would dissolve. The classroom would become the world.

• Skills would not be neglected. Engaging multimedia programs would adapt to each student's learning style. Boring drills would give way to fast-paced, individualized, high-interest skill development activities. Static textbooks would gather dust, replaced by dynamic, always-up-to-date learning resources.

• Computer technology would also revolutionize the classroom structure. Teachers would learn alongside their students. They would be facilitators of student self-learning, not purveyors of a one-size-fits-all curriculum. Test scores would soar, or tests would disappear altogether, as newly engaged, motivated students acquired skills, problem-solving abilities, and a newfound thirst for knowledge.

That was technology's promise. The reality, so far, has fallen short. Throughout the 1990s and the early years of this decade, test scores have barely budged. Textbooks are still far and away the major instructional medium. Dropout rates have remained steady. Technology's bold promises have been broken. I wondered why, and I wondered how those broken promises could be fulfilled. How could we fix the "technology fix" our schools seemed to find themselves in: billions spent for little, if any, measurable gain?

I knew I could not find the answer in books alone. I could talk to experts at universities, nonprofit think tanks, and school administrative offices, but in my view, the real experts are the kids in classrooms and the teachers who work with them every day. I needed to see things up close. To answer my question about school technology, I would have to go into classrooms. And I couldn't go only to blue ribbon schools, to acknowledged technological leaders, or to schools that were nearby and convenient. I knew I needed to visit schools across the socioeconomic and geographic spectrum: rural, suburban, and urban; rich, poor, and in between; north, south, east, and west; elementary, middle, and high schools.

Because a survey of such broad scope would take a lot of time, I took a year off from my current position. In January, after my holiday read of *The Tipping Point,* I began planning for a sabbatical. By May, my plans were in place, my job covered, and my study mapped. In addition to visiting classrooms in Massachusetts, New Hampshire, Pennsylvania, North Carolina, Ohio, Georgia, and northern and southern California, I would saturate myself in the literature of technology, learning theory, and instructional design. I would also meet with university professors from Harvard, Stanford, and Indiana Universities and attend major educational technology conferences.

I started my study with a narrowly posed question: Why, with all the resources that have been invested in technology, do the measurable results appear to be so meager? Implicit in that question were two assumptions: first, that the measurable results *were* meager, and second, that such results could be, or even should be, measurable.

The reality of schools today is that they are all about measurement. Whether one supports or opposes the standards movement and the testing that accompanies it, it is impossible to ignore that testing drives school behavior and finances. Logically, unless the billions invested in school technology over the past two decades have measurably improved student performance, I do not believe we can expect future investment to approach this level.

► ► ►

What did I learn over my year of classroom visits? Well, I learned that my narrow question about the paltry measurable performance improvements has a pretty simple answer: Students don't spend enough time on computers to make a measurable difference in performance. The average student spends about an hour a week with a computer at school. Many spend far less. A few spend more, particularly high school students who take computer-related courses such as C++ programming, computer-based accounting, or computer graphics.

There is a popular but unsupported notion that computers are used widely and constantly. Surveys report one computer for every five students. Simple math suggests that a computer could be available five hours a week for each student. But these numbers are deceptive. The count includes numerous legacy computers, machines with only marginal value. Many computers are in teachers' hands and available to students on only a limited basis, if at all. Many other computers remain turned off.

During my school visits, I walked the halls and tallied computers. Rarely did I find more than one in five in use. These were informal counts, but I consistently observed that, at any given time, 80 percent of classroom computers sat unused. Computers in labs were used more fully and were scheduled for 80 to 90 percent of class periods. But scheduled time and actual use time can be quite different. Out of every 45-minute lab class, a significant amount of time is occupied with signing on to the machine, locating the appropriate program, and shutting down before the bell rings. Under these circumstances, how much measurable effect on performance can we expect from the average hour-a-week of computer time that students have?

There is, of course, a larger question: What applications will schools find so valuable that teachers and administrators will ensure that each child uses a computer more than an hour a week? I came away with some thoughts about that, which I discuss in the final chapter.

The rest of this book chronicles my journey. I began my study in May, visited a summer program and several year-round schools during the summer months, and traveled to the balance of schools from September through February. In every school, I saw things that I admired and things that concerned me. I want to present what I saw to you: a mosaic of computer use, misuse, and nonuse. I want you to see and understand the context in which school technology is being used. After a couple of months visiting schools, I came to see that computers are used in five distinct but interrelated ways: as teaching machines, as productivity tools, as Internet portals, as data processors, and as testing devices. I discuss these uses in Chapter 21. The lines between these uses are not always sharp and will blur even further in the future, but at present, I think they provide a relevant framework.

The order in which I present these schools does not reflect the chronology of my visits, but my conclusions on the effectiveness with which the schools use technology. For organizational purposes, I have grouped the chapters into four categories:

• Schools where there was strong leadership and computer use was focused on well-defined outcomes;

- Schools where there was strong leadership but the focus on defined outcomes was less clear;

- Schools whose efforts seemed dissipated by a lack of focus, poor top-level support, or transient technology problems; and

- Schools that had severe technology, financial, or societal problems.

The demarcation lines between the groups are not always clear, but the groupings serve to organize a continuum across which school technology programs lie. In all of these schools, irrespective of my category designation, the value of technology was hampered by constraints of time, space, training, and the complexity of current hardware and software.

▶ ▶ ▶

In my travel descriptions, I do not use the actual names of schools or people. Principals, teachers, and technology coordinators welcomed me into their schools. They allowed me to see their serious problems as well as their successes. I think of them as friends and do not want to abuse their trust. Nor do I use the actual names of software programs, with the exception of the Windows Office Suite and several programs that I mention only once. By using product names, I could be more direct—and could avoid some occasional, awkward constructions that result from trying to describe a program in depth without using its commercial name— but I also could appear biased in favor of or against a particular product. I saw two programs with committed users in a number of schools. One was a reading motivation program that rewarded students for the number of books they read. Another more expensive program that I observed closely in three schools was a foundation-supported systematic instruction program. It was used with focused purpose and apparent success. I need to point out that I came away from the study convinced that software programs alone do not work magic; trained and involved teachers with superior software tools do.

In this book, I use the terms "technology" and "computers" interchangeably. That is a little sloppy, I know. To be accurate, print is a technology, as is the chalkboard, the video player, the interactive white board, the overhead projector, and any number of other support materials. But in terms of investment and use, computers are the primary technological tools, so I use the terms without distinction here.

I began my trip with no intention of turning it into a book; I was simply doing it for my own selfish reasons: I wanted to know. Also, it's worth noting that I approached this project with a pretty neutral point of view. I had no particular ax to grind, no position to defend. But to quote Pete Adams of Sunset Hills High School (see Chapter 9), "We come here with a history." As stated, my history includes a love of technology and computers, which are central to my working and leisure life. I came believing that teachers must be listened to, that strong institutions depend upon strong leadership, and that computer systems are exceedingly complex. That's my history; those are my prejudices. They come through in what I saw and conclude, but I don't think they invalidate what I am saying.

Though I went out to schools with a narrow question—how does technology influence performance?—what I observed offered a broader testimony. I saw some inspired and committed administrators shaping visions for the future and encouraging new ways of thinking and learning. I saw dedicated teachers committed to their students, trying mightily to drive the imagination, build critical-thinking skills, and equip students for this new century. I saw the other kinds of administrators and teachers too: weary, wary, and waiting for retirement, summer vacation, or the weekend. I saw bright-eyed children, fun-loving adolescents, and serious and accomplished high school students. I also saw kids with listless eyes and languid stares; others whose hyperactivity turned a chair into a constantly moving platform; and kids with baggy shirts, low-hung pants, playing gangsta or sometimes not just playing. At the close of each chapter, I offer some reflections on what I saw and felt. Implicit in them are several recommendations, which I make more explicit in Chapter 22.

Finally, the schools I visited were a microcosm of our society, reflecting all of society's victories and its painful, terrible inequalities. Go with me into those classrooms. Sit with me and listen to Cheryl Putnam as she gently welcomes a shy new child into her classroom. Join me in the back of Ramona Austin's class as her high school students discuss data structures for an Oracle database. Stand with me in the school hallway as Roberta Koughlin tells me, "Computers are a help in life. School today isn't about life, it's about proficiencies." Overhear, as I did, an inner-city mother telling her child's teacher, "It's okay for you to smack him. I'm going to when I get him home." See the ashen-faced administrator of a technology magnet school as it enters a third straight week with its network down.

Hear, feel, and see the context in which computers are being used. Leave the schools with me at day's end, exhausted from just watching, wondering how some teachers do it and understanding why so many don't. A lot of what is in this book is not directly related to technology. However, what you'll read here shows the conditions under which technology is supposed to work and make a difference.

PART I

Commitment and Focus

Of the schools I visited, I think the five schools described in Chapters 1 through 5 make the best use of technology. All of these schools are distinguished by strong leadership and the focused use of technological resources. All but one serve low-income students. Several are committed to the use and analysis of performance data.

1

St. Mary's Elementary School

St. Mary's School is tucked on a wedge of land that abuts a university campus on the east and a manufacturing plant to the immediate west. There is no outdoor play area, and heavy traffic flows past constantly. The core of the school was built in 1906; six classrooms were added in 1954. Black marble floors grace the older portions of the building, while green and red linoleum serves the newer.

The computer configuration at St. Mary's is similar to that of many elementary schools I visited: there is a lab with 28 networked computers, plus 3 to 5 networked computers in each classroom. At St. Mary's, that works out to about 3.6 children per computer, better than the reported national average of just around 5 children per computer.

"The teachers assembled the lab computers themselves," Principal Lori Applegate tells me as we walk from her office to the computer lab. "The chairman of our technology committee, a parent, negotiated for us to buy the component parts. Not only did we save money, the teachers feel real ownership. The computers are not a mystery to them."

Lori gives me the details. During a hot week in August almost two years prior to my visit, a group of nine teachers spent two days assembling the computers in the lab. Pam McDonald, the school's tech coordinator, presented the teachers with neat piles of memory chips, motherboards, power supplies, keyboards, cases, CD-ROM drives, and speakers, and then she walked them through the assembly and testing of each machine. The computers were then plugged into a prelaid cable linked to the nearby university's high-speed fiber-optic network.

"Josh Peterson, a sophomore at the university and a St. Mary's graduate, planned our system. He persuaded the university to let us tap into their network," Lori says. "These lab computers are very fast, but the classroom computers are another matter. They're hand-me-downs from school families or castoffs from local businesses."

Each teacher has a laptop, owned by the school but available for the teacher's exclusive use. A parent in the computer business arranged for each teacher to have a free Internet connection at home.

As we look around the room of 4th graders, I ask Lori if she had had any apprehensions about making this commitment to technology. "Three things worried me in the beginning, but they don't now," she replies.

"First, I was afraid that students might be isolated from one another when they were on the computers. That's not happened. Notice the buzz in this room. They help one another when they get stuck," Lori says, "and they collaborate on projects. But our tech coordinator, Pam, can tell you about those.

"Second, I was concerned that teachers might be uncomfortable not being the experts. It helped that computers were demystified when they put them together. But these teachers really seem comfortable being learners with the students.

"Third, I was initially worried about money, but I just decided we weren't going to let that stop us. We'd find the money, and we'd accept other people's junk to start with. 'A dog from every town' would be okay with us."

The school's move to technology started slowly. In 1996, Lori and a teacher team developed a technology plan. Then she told the entire staff that the school needed new teachers for the new technological era. "You can be those teachers," Lori told them. Some teachers did not want that role, so they moved on. Their replacements had to be committed to technology.

► ► ►

Pam McDonald, St. Mary's technology coordinator, looks away from her class of 4th graders to greet us. "We're doing three-minute typing drills," she reports. "We measure how many words per minute they can type with no more than three errors."

She sees me eyeing the cardboard shields that extend over each keyboard, hiding the students' hands from view. Pam explains that the shields are made from file folder stock and prevent students from looking at the keys. Before taking the tech coordinator job at St. Mary's, Pam was a high school business teacher. Typing is important to her. "Keyboarding skills are essential to computer use," she says. "If they don't learn good habits early, they have to unlearn bad ones in high school."

I assume that the high school St. Mary's feeds must be pleased to have students who can already type. I'm wrong. According to Pam, there is some tension. "They have a freshman typing class, and our kids don't need it. Kids from other feeder schools do, so our kids are a problem for them. They want us to drop our typing. It's been a real battle."

She goes on to share more details of her typing instruction. "Each child gets two 20-minute typing periods a week, starting in the second half of the 3rd grade. I developed my own typing curriculum. Each child has a folder with lessons in it. They go to the network, open their typing folders, and get to work."

Pam tells me that each class also has a 45-minute period weekly. "My goal is to support the teachers, not replace them. I teach typing, the teacher handles content. We want all technology classes to tie directly to curriculum. This is not a place for fun and—"

A bell interrupts Pam, but I know what she was going to say next. I went to a parochial school, where "no fun-and-games" was a way of life. The 5th graders close their folders, saving their work to the network. As the 5th grade students make their way out of the room, the 6th grade class streams in. They are working on end-of-year reports for social studies.

Andrea Jordan, their teacher, explains that this is a cross-curricular team project. She organized teams of four or five members. With Pam's help, she found Web sites that dealt with Roman and Greek cultures. "We studied this early in the year," Andrea says, "but I think it is very important for students to understand the roots of Western civilization. That's why I do this project as a wrap-up.

"I didn't study much about Greece and Rome until I was in college," she continues. "I felt lost in a lot of literature and history classes. I don't want my kids to have that same problem. So I require each team to research some aspect of Greece or Rome and report on it to the class. They can use books, the Web sites that Pam and I found, or any other resources. The reports can be research papers, dramatizations, PowerPoint presentations—I let the groups choose. Before they start, we go over a scoring system, or rubric, that I developed. They know what I'm looking for: good research, organization, and imagination. They get report card points for how well their team does, and each gets points for how well he or she works as a team member."

I stroll around the room, checking out the computer set-ups and looking over students' shoulders as they work. In most cases boys work with boys, girls with girls. One group of boys is working on a dramatization of Caesar's assassination, and they're discussing ways to make fake blood.

The computers line the perimeter of the classroom, their screens visible from any point. "It's the only way to arrange them," Pam tells me. "If I can't see the screens, the kids will play games or figure out how to send instant messages. Many of these kids have computers at home, and they instant-message their friends all the time. We can't let them waste time."

"They waste a lot of time when they do research at home," Andrea interjects. "Kids get distracted easily, so they do their research here, where I can watch. Then they have to find a print source from the library or home to confirm what they find on the Internet."

"We want them to understand that just because something is on the Internet doesn't make it true," Pam explains. "We want them to be critical thinkers."

As Pam says this, Lori, who had gone back to her office, reappears and joins the conversation. "Critical thinking is really essential," she confirms. "There is so much information available on the Internet that adults, not just kids, have to learn how to evaluate sources."

Andrea, half listening to us, half watching the kids, says, "Ancient history is a good topic to show this because there can be differences among the sources about dates or spellings. And to help with critical thinking, Lori will be hiring a part-time teacher for next year. She'll help us infuse critical thinking and better research skills into the curriculum, not just with technology but with everything."

"Let me show you the rest of the school," Lori offers, as we leave the lab and climb the marble-stepped staircase with its iron railings. I ask if I can look into the classrooms to see how those computers are being used. We look in one classroom after another. In all but two, the computers are turned off. In one 3rd grade classroom, four students sit at computers. "They finished a vocabulary test early," the teacher tells us, "so they can play games. Educational games, of course."

Viewpoint

This first visit showed me the initial glimpses of themes and experiences that recurred in the months that followed. I saw that strong building leadership is essential. Principal Lori Applegate's unambiguous message to teachers was "Get on the train or get off."

Strong principals hire strong technology coordinators who share their vision.

I also saw that a coordinated curriculum is essential, not only within a school but between schools. Poor coordination leads to lost time and confusion. Think of the skilled typists that St. Mary's sent on to high school—students whose keyboarding skills should have been welcome. Without a coordinated curriculum between the middle and high school, those skills, and the students who have them, become "a problem." I saw a similar lack of curriculum coordination in other schools and districts.

Finally, at St. Mary's I first saw that teachers need a sense of ownership over their school's technology program. If administrators who are distant from the classroom select the program's goals, equipment, materials, and methods, technology implementation is likely to be sluggish. The staff at St. Mary's assembled their own computers. They understood their school's technology plan and they chose to be there to implement it. In my school visits, I saw a number of schools that had yet to implement programs purchased by the central office two or three years earlier. Teachers either didn't know these programs existed or had received only superficial orientation about how to use them. Without buy-in at the classroom level, technology investment simply does not pay off.

▶ ▶ ▶ *2*

Harriet Tubman Elementary School

ON A SWELTERING DAY IN MID-JULY, I PULL INTO THE PARKING lot of Harriet Tubman Elementary School. Summer session is on at this school, which borders a major midwestern city. Harriet Tubman, originally called Cherry Park School, was renamed two years ago. The neighborhood population is predominantly black and very transient. Many of the area's large, single-family homes have been converted into low-income apartments and rooming houses.

As I enter the school, I hear and feel the effects of two giant fans, one at each end of the central corridor. It is only 7:45 a.m., and the heat and humidity are already beginning to build. The fans may rearrange that heat, but I suspect they will do little to eliminate it.

On my way to the office, I pass walls of trophy cases and notice that every case contains books. I hear footsteps in the corridor— loud, authoritative, quick. They belong to Principal Peter Malone, who approaches, hand extended, beads of sweat already forming on his forehead. Peter was a reading specialist in the district until he took the Harriet Tubman job three years ago. When I comment on trophy cases full of books, Peter explains, "This school is all about reading. If our kids don't learn to read, they won't learn science, social studies, math. It is the basis of everything they do. We keep drumming that into the kids and their parents. Reading is our number-one priority."

▶ ▶ ▶

That priority explains the heavy investment Peter has made in a computer-based reading program. Now in its third year at the school, the program was developed with support from the federal government and nonprofit foundations. It carries the very high price tag of about $25,000 per classroom, which includes the specially equipped, high-powered computers needed to run the multimedia-packed program.

For Harriet Tubman Elementary School, the price was even higher. Because the program is available only for PCs, Peter had to replace his year-old Apple lab with Windows equipment. Peter was so convinced that the new reading program was vital to his students' success that he bit the bullet and made the switch.

Peter's school system has a strong site-based management tradition. As principal, Peter receives about $7,000 per student, and with a few exceptions, he can budget the money how he thinks best. To fund the program, Peter knew he would need to beg, borrow, and swipe from other budget categories.

School district funds alone could not support the reading program purchase. Peter also used Title I funds and a $10,000 grant from a suburban church. The church members once lived in the Harriet Tubman neighborhood and now support the school with volunteer tutors as well as financial aid.

"Has the program been successful?" I ask Peter.

"Yes, but if you are looking for hard data, I can't really give it to you," he tells me. "Data evaporates with our turnover of more than 35 percent a year. At the end of three years, only a handful of the students who began the program in kindergarten are still enrolled here. So I can't document the progress that I know is there.

"Come with me, and I'll let you see for yourself," he says as he strides toward a classroom up the corridor. "You'll see the individual attention the computer gives. Computers are infinitely patient. They don't get frustrated like I do. There is no way we could give the kind of attention this program offers."

▶ ▶ ▶

We enter a classroom, where four 1st and 2nd graders sit at computers. Two of them are at tables facing the wall. The other two are at tables facing the center of the room. Two children sit at another table quietly reading or looking at picture books. A young teacher sits at yet another table with two more children. They are reading to her in turns from a colorfully illustrated paperback.

"We won't interrupt her," Peter says, nodding toward the teacher, Susan Meyer. "She's expecting you, so just feel at home. Look at what the kids are doing. I'm going back to the office and will see you later."

Peter leaves, and I walk quietly across the room and stop several feet behind a young girl named La'nasha. She looks up, smiles a shy hello, and turns her attention back to the computer. She has her finger on the screen and is tracing it over the letter M. Her lips are pursed as her finger moves with a graceful curving motion up, across, down, up, across, down. "Mmmm," I hear her saying. "Mmmm."

At a computer next to her, a little boy named Lindell sits listlessly, head cradled on the palm of his left hand, right hand on the mouse. His posture says boredom, but only briefly, as he suddenly makes a victory gesture, pounding one hand into another and crying, "Yes!"

"Lindell," Susan admonishes quietly, not looking away from the students before her at the table.

Energized by his apparent success, Lindell looks again at the screen, gets up and walks to a nearby printer, waits for a page to come out, selects a pencil from a can beside the printer, and returns to his seat. The computer table is large enough for him to work with the paper comfortably.

I look at the sheet. It is titled "Lindell's Writing Words." There are two columns on the sheet, one of words ending with -*ill* (pill, hill, fill, drill, mill, gill), the other with words ending with -*int* (hint, mint, tint, print, lint). Carefully he prints each word, holds up the paper, and says, "Beautiful."

From behind me, I hear, "Slush, slug, slip, slim." La'nasha is reading into a small microphone. She reads from a list of words on the screen, and her recorded voice plays back through earphones. Then the screen fades and the name "Marian Wright" appears. La'-nasha gets up, walks over to a table, and taps the shoulder of a little girl who is reading a book. This must be Marian, who gets up and moves to the computer.

At the table in the center of the room, Susan listens attentively as two students take turns reading. They read slowly, carefully: "'I . . . am . . . sad, . . . said . . . Sam." The little girl looks up at the teacher. Her eyes ask, "Did I get it right?" Susan gives a gentle smile and says, "Good, Tanya. Now you read, Maurice."

As Maurice starts to read, another child approaches the table and taps Tanya for her turn at the computer. Tanya moves silently to the computer with her name on the screen. She clicks the mouse on "Start" in the lower right-hand corner, and the cover of a book appears.

Maurice has finished reading, and Susan has a short break, so we talk. This is her third year of teaching, she tells me. She likes the computer reading program. "It tells me a lot about how the kids are doing. The computer helps me, but it doesn't take over. I still get to teach and monitor progress. It is important for these kids that I listen to their reading. The program helps them with basics in a way I couldn't do by myself, especially during the school year, when I'd have 20 to 25 kids here, not 8."

Susan wears knee-length shorts and a white, short-sleeved blouse. The summer's heat is starting to fill the room. The windows are open, but the hall fans stir no breeze. "They'd rather be outside playing," she says, nodding to the children in the class, "but their parents want them here, and the kids like the computers and the attention I can give them. We recommend about 30 percent of the kids for this summer program—the ones who showed problems in kindergarten or 1st grade. About 80 percent of the kids we recommend actually come. We think that's pretty good. Peter works hard with the parents, stressing how reading is the key to future success at school and in life."

▸ ▸ ▸

Principal Peter Malone comes to the door of the classroom and motions to me. I join him in the hall, where he stands with a boy, about 4th grade level. Peter has a paper filled with numbers in his hand. "This is Randall, and this is his reading record. I want to show it to you," Peter says.

Randall looks at me, eyes shining. "Tell Mr. Pflaum what you did today," Peter prompts.

"I got my 25 points! I mean, I got my baseball tickets. Me and my mom are going to a game," Randall says excitedly.

Peter explains that the school uses a reading motivation program that awards children points for the books they read independently. When a child accumulates 25 point, they receive two tickets to a major league baseball game.

Peter shows me Randall's record sheet. It lists the books he has read, their level, their level-based point value, and Randall's total: 25.1 points. "This last book you read is only 2.6 points," Peter says to Randall. "You can read 4th grade books."

"I know," Randall says earnestly, "but I needed to finish a book by today to get the tickets." Randall was obviously good at math, too.

Peter explains that some teachers and librarians object to the motivation program. And some librarians don't like assigning levels to books because they fear that kids won't reach beyond their current comfort zone to explore more challenging books. Peter understands these objections but says that he is primarily interested in the results: It's summer, and Randall is reading.

As Randall and Peter head to the office to get the baseball tickets, I go to another classroom. There are nine children in the class, a mix of 1st and 2nd graders. The teacher is Janet Zimmerman, a woman in her 50s, who is new to primary reading instruction. Telling two children to continue on their own, she joins me just inside the door.

"I taught 5th and 6th grade math for nearly 20 years," she tells me. "I was ready for a change, and Peter convinced me I could do this. It's an adjustment to work with these younger children, but I like them and I like working with the computer reading program. I like data analysis, and the program gives me lots of data to work with."

Earlier I had asked Peter how teachers took to the use of data. "Some better than others," he said, "but I tell them the computer has two virtues. It is patient and it is precise. The program's virtue is that it does what it does best and allows the teacher to focus her teaching based on the computer's information. Teachers still teach; the computer helps."

► ► ►

At 11:45 a.m., the dismissal bell rings and the hall fills with chattering kids. Peter stands at the school door, releasing one group at a time: "Have a great afternoon. . . . Stay cool. . . . See you tomorrow. . . . Read that book. . . . I hope your team wins." He has a personal farewell for each child and for many of the waiting parents.

"Parent contact is essential," he tells me after the children have gone. "It's hard here. Many of the parents have two jobs. A lot have none. They move constantly. They move out here, then back downtown, then back out here, a step ahead of, or behind, the rent collector. It's hard to maintain continuity. But we keep trying, and some of it sticks. We just keep trying."

Viewpoint

When I think back on Harriet Tubman Elementary, I'm reminded of a book by Stanford education professor Larry Cuban. In the book, *Oversold and Underused,* Cuban critiques the standards and technology movements. Both movements, he points out, originated outside the educational establishment; the standards movement was sparked by business leaders worried about their next generation of workers, and the technology movement was promoted by companies interested in selling hardware and software.

Too much focus, Cuban writes, has been placed on schools as engines of a private, individualistic economy, and too little focus has been placed on schools' broader social purpose of serving and building communities. But Cuban has not met Principal Peter Malone; he hasn't seen the intensity in Peter's eyes or heard the commitment in his voice. He has not seen the low-income parents bringing children to school on a sweltering summer day because Peter has convinced them that reading is essential for their kids' futures.

At Harriet Tubman, technology was used well: in small groups with focused purpose and careful teacher support and interaction. I saw teachers who were comfortable analyzing and applying computer-produced data. I saw students motivated to read by a computer-supported incentive program. I saw a computer-based management system that served the teacher, not one that turned the teacher into a servant of technology. At Harriet Tubman, technology seemed to be working in these classes of eight or nine students. How would it work in classes of 20, 25, or even 30? Before long, I found out.

3

Longworth
High School

I'M STANDING AT THE FRONT OF A HIGH SCHOOL CLASSROOM. Before me, I see 18 faces. Fifteen are black. Three belong to girls. When I ask why they are taking this class in Oracle programming, the students reply, "To make money. Lots of it." Their teacher, Ramona Austin, stands in the back, a slight smirk on her face.

Ramona is the technology coordinator for Longworth High School, a 2,200-student urban school in a major city in the Southeast. Longworth is a technology magnet school, and 80 percent of the students have chosen to be here.

Ramona also teaches the Oracle programming class that I'm observing. Today's lesson is about data structures. She asks me to speak with the class about opportunities in the business world. I've just watched my company install an Oracle system with the help of an army of highly paid programmers and consultants, so I feel prepared to talk about the opportunities for Oracle programmers.

These students don't need encouragement. They are serious, bright, and good-naturedly combative. "What's the biggest challenge in this class?" I ask, wanting to gauge their commitment.

"The network is down 25 percent of the time," one of the three white students in the class volunteers.

"No way! No way! How can you say that?" a chorus of voices responds.

There is a solid consensus that 2 or 3 percent downtime is more like it. Ramona confirms that records show downtime in that range. "Other challenges?" I prompt.

"I don't have a computer at home. I can't get the homework done," a male voice calls from the back of the room.

"Get off that," a girl reacts with a sharp verbal slap. "You're just making excuses. If you want computer time, you can get it. Get out of bed and get here before school. Go to a library. Don't give us that—"

"Enough," Ramona says as she walks to the front of the room. She's now in charge, and I take her place in the back.

"Jamal, get that pillow out of this classroom." Ramona has spotted the pillow that I saw wedged under the desk of a young man in the second row.

"It's for lunch," he protests. "I won't use it in class. I was up all night working. I'm sleeping at lunch, not here."

Ramona relents and continues the lesson on data structures that began earlier in the week. The class is studying the relationship between entities in a retail database. A vigorous discussion unfolds over questions like, "What are the attributes of a product?" and, "What is the relationship between customer number and product number?"

A gangly student slouches in his seat, his baggy pants draped nearly to the floor, his hair braided into cornrows, a bandana tied around his head. With a verbal swagger, he argues that a certain term is an "item," not a "product," as Ramona insists. Every time she says "product," he challenges her with "item." He's testing. This is as much about power as it is about data structures. But he is obviously smart and engaged. Ramona concedes that he has a point, and the class moves on.

She asks for homework, and most of the students pull papers from folders or daypacks. "Have you did it?" one student asks another in a voice that all can hear. "Have you *done* it," corrects the girl who slapped back earlier. I think to myself that she'll be in charge somewhere someday.

▶ ▶ ▶

Longworth High School uses block scheduling, with 90-minute classes twice a week. Forty-five minutes have passed, and Ramona moves on to student presentations. She tells the class that, as database programmers, they will have to defend their data structures to clients or colleagues. Presentation skills are important, she emphasizes, reminding the class that the rubric she uses to grade presentations is on her Web site.

The first presentation is by a young man who heads a team of three student programmers working on a computer game animation. He describes how they planned the animation and wrote the 300,000 lines of code to date. He expects the total program to be more than 1,000,000 lines. *Who has to follow this presentation?* I wonder.

I won't find out because Ramona has me scheduled to visit a world civilizations class. As I make my way there, I look into rooms where classes are going on. Three teachers are using overhead projectors; computers sit unused. I find the world civilizations room. The teacher, Arlan Watson, is expecting me. He nods as I enter the room and move to the back.

The classroom is crowded, with students sitting in traditional student chairs. Many read newspaper clippings cut from their family newspaper. A third of the students have newspapers open and are marking or tearing out articles on world events. Several are without newspapers or clippings. Six computers sit unused in the back of the room.

Taking turns, students describe the events covered by their articles. On a wall map, they point to the locations where their stories originated. "I'm trying to get them to understand what takes place beyond the limited world they know," Arlan explains to me as I prepare to leave.

▶ ▶ ▶

Ramona had expected this to be a technology-supported class. When she laid out my visit itinerary earlier in the day, she explained that Longworth has 2,200 students and about 600 computers, a ratio of 3.7 to 1. Each humanities classroom has six computers; math and science rooms have between two and eight. The school urges teachers to integrate technology into their core instruction. "As technology coordinator," Ramona told me, "I spend about a third of my time on staff development, teaching programs like PowerPoint or Excel. Mostly I try to help teachers on a one-to-one basis."

Many of Longworth's computers are in labs. Three are open labs, where teachers sign up on a first-come, first-served basis. There is a Cisco lab for courses leading to certification as a Cisco network technician; the Oracle lab I visited earlier, where C++ programming is also taught; a business studies lab for keyboarding, accounting, and other business subjects; a marketing lab; a computer-aided design (CAD) lab; and a media center with 40 workstations. Each lab has about 30 computers.

A local community college uses the computer labs in the evenings. Longworth students can earn double benefit from these courses, which count toward high school graduation and as college credit.

Federal grants supported Longworth's initial wiring and hardware and software acquisition. Replacing these now-aging computers will cost the school about $300,000 a year, but this year's budget allocates only $10,000 for materials.

Ramona wears many hats and is driven by her belief in technology's value to instruction and to the futures of Longworth's students. She worries, though, about how shrinking budgets could choke off upgrades and replacements. Ramona was a humanities student in college, taught elementary school, earned a media specialist's graduate degree, worked in video production, served as a high school librarian, and took a technology coordinator's job at an underperforming elementary school.

There, she discovered the power of technology to dramatically increase measured performance. The school adopted a systematic program of computer instruction. Passing rates on state tests rose from 31 percent to 89 percent. Ramona is convinced that computer instruction was the single variable that accounted for the school's success.

Longworth was still on the drawing board when Ramona accepted the position of director of technology instructional support. She brought to her job energy, experience, and unwavering faith in technology's impact. She has a staff of three and a handful of student volunteers.

In addition to her other responsibilities, Ramona tends to the needs of the humanities faculty. A second technology staff member, who has a reduced teaching load, supports math and science, and a third, also with a reduced teaching load, supports instruction in the media lab. A separate technology management team provides hardware, network, and infrastructure support. That team also staffs the technology labs, one of which I visit after the world civilizations class.

► ► ►

I walk into the computer lab and find Larry Purcell. Larry, who teaches 9th grade math, has signed up for a 90-minute lab period. He is teaching Algebra I to lower-performing students assigned to the class based on their 8th grade scores. The class is working on several Microsoft Excel activities. One involves entering the heights and weights of professional basketball players and comparing their height-to-weight ratios. Another involves using a spreadsheet to compute the total and the average cost of textbooks.

I ask Larry about his opinion of the benefits of technology and his reasons for taking time for Excel activities. How do such activities fit into his algebra instruction?

"Not very well," he acknowledges, but he believes that "kids have to know this in today's world." I look around and see that the students, even numbers of girls and boys, seem involved in the activity. In pairs, they are puzzling over the proper keystrokes and mouse clicks to enter data and compose simple formulas.

"Some kids come here from middle school knowing a little about Excel. I teach it to the ones who don't. I'm thinking about their futures. This doesn't help them all that much now, in algebra class or out," he explains. "We're known as the technology school, but we really only have three labs we can use. We really can't do all that much."

I drift over to speak with a lab aide, Mae Johnson. While I was speaking with Larry, she had been busy with a student, carrying on a conversation that seemed more argument than talk. Now that she's free, I ask what she does in her job, how she came into the job, and what its challenges are.

Mae manages the lab and supports teachers and students when they run into hardware or software problems. She also checks the planner of each student who enters the lab. That's what the "discussion" with the student had been about.

Every Longworth student carries a calendar planner that holds basic information about the student, including whether he or she is an authorized computer user. To use any school computer, students and their parents must sign the school's Authorized Use Policy (AUP). The AUP spells out strict guidelines for computer use and protects the district from liability in case of misuse. Each day, when students enter the lab, Mae checks their planners to verify that the AUP is signed. If it is not, the student is denied computer access. Today, a boy whose parents disapprove of computer use because of concern over Internet content sits reading a book. "Most parents will sign," Mae explains, "but the forms get lost or the planners are left at home or in the student's car. There are lots of issues and problems."

▶ ▶ ▶

Adjoining this computer lab is another like it. I enter the second lab and introduce myself to Howard Matthews, an advanced placement biology teacher. The 30 computers are in 4 parallel rows of 7 or 8 each. The room is hushed, the students in serious thought. Most of the computer screens show an online test with multiple-choice items and several open-ended essay questions. Howard developed the exam, which covers cell biology, using a test program he downloaded from the Internet. This program will automatically correct the multiple-choice questions and save the essays for Howard to grade individually.

"These are bright kids," Howard says as we step into the hall. "I organize them into teams of two and have each team develop a Web site covering the cell biology topics we're studying. Everything we do is project-based, so I only give short lectures. They do the rest.

"They really get into these Web sites," he adds. "They work on them late at night, communicating with one another over the Net about what they are finding. They share the Web sites here in class. Because they've done the research, they know they can trust the information on their sites. I make them cite the source of any information or graphics, of course. When they obtain information from sites that I'm not acquainted with, we discuss the criteria for determining site reliability.

"These kids are independent thinkers," Howard continues. "I push them and tell them to go beyond advanced high school biology. They should think of themselves now as college students. They are on the cusp. At some point, Web sites like these will lose their attraction. Already the kids are moving beyond: animating cell division and mitosis or tracking developments in cancer research. I'm at home with technology, but I learn a lot from them."

▶ ▶ ▶

The class period ends, and the students save, shut down, and leave. A new group files into the lab. This is a vocabulary development class, a semester-long English elective for lower-performing freshmen. Counselors recommend it for students who have undeveloped language skills. The teacher, Gordon Phillips, tells me that many of the students are bright but have had meager language exposure at home and in their earlier schooling.

"Vocabulary is the key to reading and learning, and we work here to build their vocabularies," he tells me. Gordon has taught both Greek and Latin. The first half of this course covers words with Greek and Latin origins. The second half covers the languages of professions such as medicine and law. He developed the course outline himself and creates many of the course materials. He uses a paperbound vocabulary development book and brings the students to the lab to search the Internet for examples of vocabulary usage.

Gordon is new at Longworth and enthused by its technology and its attitude: "These are poor minority kids, but they are very motivated. The attitude from the top down is that everyone here will succeed. Kids take pride in what they do on computers."

I wonder where this can-do attitude originated, and find the answer in Robert Sims, Longworth's principal. Robert would fit comfortably into the corporate world, speaking the language of customer service, team-based organization, and strategic planning. But of course, those corporate concepts have now seeped (or is it flooded?) into education.

"Take away the technology, and there is no reason for our kids to be here," Robert tells me. "It would vastly change what this school is. Over three-quarters of our students are here by choice. We offer something that is vital to their futures. Technology is their future and ours."

► ► ►

Before I leave Longworth, I visit another class and meet individually with the supervisors of humanities and math/science. These women oversee the curriculum and manage the selection of teaching materials. They explain to me that time is one of their most precious commodities. When computers save time, they are good. When they take up time, they are bad.

What advantages do electronic books have over printed books? None that they can see. Computerized tests over printed tests? Computerized tests correct themselves—and thus save time. What about the CD-ROMs or Web-based supplements that accompany textbooks? Do they want them and use them? Sometimes, they tell me. They give the example of a literature program that offers a CD-ROM with poems by Robert Frost and other poets who are not in the anthology text.

"Some very good CD-ROMs accompany our grammar and composition textbooks," the humanities supervisor tells me. She roots through a large box of ancillaries and pulls out two CDs. They are still shrink-wrapped, unopened and unused. "There is just too much to look at and not enough time," she says by way of explanation.

Viewpoint

Longworth High School was impressive. The kids, most of whom were from ethnic minority backgrounds, received a clear message of hope delivered by teachers and administrators who believed in them and in technology. But could the staff's belief in the students prevail over the seemingly inevitable budget cuts that will shrink the school's technology funds? Is the essential pull of a magnet school like Longworth the technology instruction it provides? Or is it really the staff, with their insistence that these kids have bright futures?

When I think of Longworth, I also remember the humanities supervisor and her unopened CD-ROMs. As the year progressed, I saw additional evidence that teachers are burdened less by a lack of available software than by its surfeit. The software supply far exceeds demand, which is shaped by the amount of time teachers have available to evaluate, learn about, and use the software they already possess.

At Longworth, I encountered dynamic leadership, an outstanding technological infrastructure, and strong technical and curricular support for technology users. But I saw only a few software programs in use: productivity programs like Word and Excel, and Front Page—used for Web site development in the advanced placement biology class. In addition, the Web was used as an important information source in a variety of classes.

At other schools, technology coordinators and teachers told me they had little time to become well acquainted with available instructional programs that support content and skill acquisition, as opposed to productivity programs. Often, I found teachers were not thoroughly versed in the content of the programs they assigned. They chose programs based on word of mouth or limited exposure at inservice workshops. Programs on a school or district server, which carried with them an implicit endorsement, were often assigned as free-time work, even if the teachers didn't know the programs well or understand how they correlated to the curriculum. The value of such programs to students is hit or miss. This surfeit of materials combined with the limited time available for teachers to evaluate, learn about, and use them explains the falloff in software sales over the past several years. The rise in Internet use, too, has contributed to that sales stagnation. Such a decline also points to something more important: the shift away from the computer's role as teaching machine and toward its role as information source, productivity tool, and data processor (see Chapter 21).

4

▶ ▶ ▶

Washington-Connors Elementary School

SNOW SPECKLES MY WINDSHIELD AS I PULL AWAY FROM THE Rainbow Diner east of Randolph, Ohio, a struggling river town downstream from chemical and coke processing plants. The plants, some now rusted and abandoned, are fed by the cross-river coal mines of Kentucky and West Virginia. Nearby is a shuttered nuclear processing plant that shed more than 1,000 jobs during the 1990s.

Leaving Randolph, I follow 12 miles of twisting roads through the hollows of Wilson County, searching for the school I'm to visit. Highway 5 snakes through the hills, past intersecting roads with names like Campbell Furnace, Salt Lick, and Dawson Hope. A chilly mist hangs over the patchy fields. Trailers, cabins, and small barns— one converted into a house—dot the nearby fields. The rising sun peeks between the hills, illuminating a sign: Washington School, Washington-Connors School District. My appointment with Jack Hayward, the principal, is at 8:00 a.m.

Washington-Connors is one of Ohio's poorest districts, with the 12th-lowest income out of more than 600 districts. Its largest town is Horton Center, population 790. Only a few cars sit in the school's lot. I think to myself, *Maybe school starts late and the principal wants to see me before students arrive.* I try the nearest door. It's locked. So is a second. A third opens, and I step in quietly.

The school is old, but it has a familiar feel for someone who went to grade school in the 1940s. At the top of the stairs, I find myself in a large, high-ceilinged classroom. Boxes line the walls, and four students sit before computers at an island of tables in the middle. A heavyset young man in his early 20s oversees them from a chair off to the side.

"I'm looking for Jack Hayward," I tell him.

"You won't find him here," he answers. "He's at Washington-Connors, over in Horton Center. You're at the old Washington School. This place is for special programs like this SBH [Severely Behaviorally Handicapped] class. They do Head Start and Even Start here, too."

After new directions and a 15-minute drive, I reach my destination. In contrast to the school I've just left, the building before me is modern, low to the ground. It is downhill from a similarly designed high school, and this campus setting speaks of money—lots of it.

▶ ▶ ▶

I enter the elementary building and quickly find Principal Jack Hayward. Tall and athletic, his bearing says "coach" more than "principal." A veteran school administrator, Jack has been in the district for four years. "Before that, I was principal at Dawson Elementary," he tells me. "We were a U.S. Office of Education blue ribbon school. Larry Sowder, our superintendent here in Washington-Connors, asked me to come help plan this new school. I started as curriculum director, but a lot of my time was spent planning and building this place."

The Washington-Connors Elementary School cost $12 million, Jack says. The state paid 95 percent of that. Because of Washington-Connors's meager tax base and poverty-level incomes, the district had to come up with only $860,000. Even that was a stretch.

The elementary school has 600 students. Another 400 attend the high school next door, which houses grades 7 through 12. Student turnover is relatively low, about 15 percent a year. Teacher turnover is even lower: In the past year, only 1 of 51 teachers left, and that was for maternity leave. Faculty come from nearby colleges in Ohio, Kentucky, and West Virginia. In the Washington-Connors School District, apples don't fall far from the tree.

The students in the school are a homogeneous group: with the exception of two biracial students, all are white. All are native English speakers. But there are plenty of challenges associated with the area's high unemployment rate, low wages, and disappearing industry.

I talk to Jack about my study of technology and performance. "Technology can be a good support system," Jack tells me, "but nothing is as important as the teachers themselves. Nothing replaces a good teacher who cares about kids."

Jack invites me to stay all day, which includes the after-school enrichment program that runs from 3:30 p.m. to 5:30 p.m. The program is funded by a grant through the state university in Randolph, and the school district gets $360,000 a year to support the program. That money is split evenly between the elementary school and the high school.

At the elementary school, 20 teachers are paid $16 an hour to conduct a variety of after-school classes, including both hard-core academics and enrichment. Every child takes one of each type. Choices range from phonics and math to T'ai Chi and chess. About 200 of the 600 kids stay for the afternoon program.

I'm especially interested in seeing the way Washington-Connors Elementary applies the instructional software I'd observed during the summer reading classes at Harriet Tubman Elementary School (see Chapter 2). I want to see how it's used in this setting, during the regular school year.

"I didn't think we'd be able to afford that program," Jack says. "But the sales representative helped us get $160,000 to support our purchase. I went with him to a state education committee hearing in Columbus. The senate president and speaker of the house both spoke in favor of funding it. I'd never seen anything like that.

"We use the program 15 minutes a day in kindergarten, then 30 minutes a day in the five 1st grade classrooms," he tells me as we walk toward one of the 1st grade rooms. Along the way, Jack's pride in the school is evident.

"The faculty helped us plan this building," he enthuses. "We sat down with the architects and teachers and talked about what we needed and what we wanted. These courtyards were the teachers' idea." Jack stops in front of a glass wall facing out onto a long, rectangular courtyard. The opposite wall faces a similar courtyard.

"This one is used for outdoor science classes." Jack describes how students measure rainfall and do other science activities here, then leads me to the other courtyard. He opens the door and takes me out to a sculpture court. Down the middle is a graceful serpentine walk. On each side, at 8- to 10-foot intervals, are narrow cement pedestals. "We have a visiting artist who teaches sculpture," Jack notes. "The students read books and sculpted pieces based on the book characters."

I notice a likeness of Harry Potter resting on one of the pedestals. "The students sculpt with clay, and then the molds are made at a forge in Randolph," Jack says. "In a couple of weeks, we'll have brass plaques with each artist's name."

▶ ▶ ▶

We reenter the building, and Jack takes me to Cheryl Putnam's 1st grade classroom.

"Come in, come in," Cheryl welcomes as I go through the doorway. Multiple bins of books rest against three classroom walls. Against the fourth wall are five computers. In the center of the room, desks sit in an oblong arrangement. Mats cover the floor, many decorated with words, numbers, and book characters. The remaining floor space is occupied by milk crates containing more books, organized and identified by reading level. Posters and banners cover the walls. At one end of the room is a Christmas tree with rocking chairs on either side.

"How many books?" I ask Cheryl.

"At last count, about a thousand," she replies. "I buy them everywhere I can. I just can't stop myself."

A classroom aide attends to the 17 students as Cheryl continues: "I didn't learn to read until I was in 4th or 5th grade. I moved a lot as a child. Never understood phonics."

I guess Cheryl to be in her mid-40s. She tells me she has been teaching for only six years. "My first year, I was an aide for an autistic child. Then I had a year with special ed, and now it's been four years in 1st grade.

"This is my love," she says, pointing to a computer screen that runs the reading motivation program I'd seen at Harriet Tubman. "Children learn to read by reading, reading, and reading. I'll do anything to get them to read. This program even has 500 narrated books. The school's bought all of them. Kids can read and listen. That helps lots of these children."

Behind me, a boy sits at a computer. On the screen are several questions, testing whether he has understood *The Birthday Car,* a book he has just read. A little girl stands by his chair. As he hesitates on a question, she coaches him impatiently. When he finishes the 10th and last question, the computer program displays his score.

"You're done," the girl says, squeezing onto the chair and edging him off. She clicks briskly through the 10 questions, smiles with satisfaction at the 100 percent score, goes to her desk, and takes out a sheet of chart paper. She fills in block 32. "That's my 32nd book," she beams.

"Do you think a child's performance on the state proficiency tests is helped by using this program?" I ask Cheryl.

"Oh, yes, 110,000 percent," she says, "Our reading program teaches them some really important things. But it's not just the programs the children use that are important. It's the information the software gives me. It tells me tons about what I do with them. The reading motivation program gives me all sorts of information, too.

Some of it I use and some I send home. Come here and let me show you."

But before she can continue, Jack returns to the room. Just behind him is a reticent little girl who looks at the floor, then back at her mother, who stands slightly inside the classroom door. The girl's name is Ariel, and it is clear that she does *not* want to be here.

"Ariel. That's a beautiful name," Cheryl says. Then she turns to the class. "This is Ariel. She's joining us today."

A boy sitting at the circle of desks tells Cheryl, "She can sit here and use my markers."

The girl, eyes still fastened to the floor, is unaware that her mother has backed into the hallway. Seventeen pairs of eyes look toward Ariel. She looks up, sees them, realizes her mother has moved, and runs out to the hall to cling to her mother's leg.

Cheryl leaves the room, takes Ariel by the hand, and gently leads her back. The mother watches apprehensively. "Sit here," she tells Ariel quietly. The boy hands Ariel a marker and a sheet of paper. Cheryl goes to the front of the class and takes over from the aide.

"God told me there would be someone to help today," Cheryl tells me later. "He's always right. God led me to be a teacher, to this school, to this class. You just have to trust in Him. He told me to accept Ariel. I really didn't want another student in here, but God wants her to be in this class."

▶ ▶ ▶

As Cheryl continues with the lesson, I find my way to another 1st grade classroom. The teacher, Carol Ludgate, has a free period while her class is at music. I want to ask her about an auditory support program she uses. The program, based upon recent neurological research, helps students discriminate among phonemic elements. I've spoken with other teachers and hearing specialists who use it, and I'd like another viewpoint.

Overall, Carol's opinion is not particularly favorable. However, she mentions that it was a big help to a student struggling to re-acquire aural discrimination ability following the removal of a brain tumor. "Jason responded very well to the program," she says. "I know he made progress when he used it."

With 24 years' experience as a 1st grade teacher, Carol is the picture of a confidence and competence. "We spent $20,000 for 50 software licenses," she says. "We can't use that many, but of course we didn't know that when we bought them. To use the program successfully, you can't have more than three children per adult. We don't have that many teachers or aides. We've never had more than 15 kids using it, but now there are only 2.

"One thing I've learned is that software doesn't work by itself. Teachers are important to the use of any software program. I really believe that. A teacher has to understand a program, and she has to feel it's important. If she doesn't feel it's important, neither will the student."

Carol obviously feels that computers are important. She has five in her room. Two are dedicated to the reading motivation program and three to the systematic reading support program that she, Cheryl Putnam, and the other primary grade teachers are using. None of Carol's five computers is connected to the Internet. "We spend so much time on reading that we don't need the Internet for the kids," she explains. "We teachers have it for research, and six teachers in this school are getting their M.A.s online."

I ask her how a 24-year veteran feels about the current focus on assessment and accountability. "What I know is that we've become too test-oriented," she tells me. "It's okay to be curriculum-oriented. We have to be aligned with standards. We can't just teach whatever we want. Some teachers always teach a butterfly unit or a dinosaur unit. If these don't match curriculum standards, they have to change."

► ► ►

The bell rings, and Carol's students file in from music class. I go up to the second floor to visit Gloria Hauser, a 3rd grade teacher who is using a computer-based math practice program.

A young girl stands by Gloria's desk, practice sheet in hand and a troubled look on her face. "I don't understand this," the girl says. "What am I supposed to do?"

"What is the question asking?" Gloria prompts, patiently.

The girl is quiet for a moment, then says, "I think I know now."

"I think you do, too," assures the teacher.

Several times during my visit, students ask for similar help. Each time, Gloria asks the same thing: "What is the question asking?"

Most students are at their desks, working in pairs. One student says to another, "You have one dollar. You pay 64 cents for a hot dog and drink. How much change do you get?"

Gloria hears the question and listens while the boy thinks. He is hesitant, having trouble. "Pretend it's a proficiency test," she advises. "Read it again and do it just like on the proficiency test. That will help you."

Gloria tells me about the computer-based math program she is using. The program doesn't teach math on screen, but instead generates a series of practice sheets that corresponds to a student's performance on a computer-based test. The test identifies areas where the student is weak and needs help, then produces practice sheets with problems focusing on the areas of weakness. Students record multiple-choice answers on scannable answer forms.

I notice a quiet buzz in the classroom. It's the buzz of thinking. It is also the buzz of the scanning machine into which students insert their filled-in answer sheets. As quickly as the machine reads the sheets, it prints out results."They love to use the scanner," Gloria tells me. "They love the immediate results. At 3rd and 4th grade, students start to take responsibility for their own learning. This program helps them do that."

▶ ▶ ▶

I return to Principal Jack Hayward's office. I'll be going to a science class next, but first I want to get some information about the school's technology plan and equipment.

"We have a lab for grades 4 through 6," Jack says. "All 4th through 6th grade classes go to the lab at least once a week. Our tech teacher is here in the mornings, then goes to the middle school in the afternoon. Teachers can sign up for the lab in the afternoon. It is used 25 to 50 percent of those available hours."

Washington-Connors Elementary is unlike most schools I have visited, where classroom computers frequently sit unused while labs are often busy. It seems just the opposite here. I'd like to find out why, but I need to move on to Anita Parker's 4th grade science class.

As I enter the room, Anita comes over, explaining that a student teacher is conducting today's lesson. Anita and I sit on two plastic lawn chairs in the classroom. Next to the chairs sits a two-person plastic couch. Hanging by strings from the ceiling are cutouts of angels decorated with markers and sequins, an art project from an earlier class period.

The student teacher stands in the middle of the classroom, the desks forming a semicircle around her. She stands in stocking feet, teaching a whole-class lesson on gases and solids. The students take turns reading from their textbooks, which carry a 1984 copyright. After each child reads, the class discusses the content. The student teacher asks why helium balloons rise but air-filled balloons do not. No one knows the answer. Neither does the student teacher. "Do teachers know everything?" she asks. She answers her own question: "No, they don't. So how would you find out?"

The student teacher tells the class to take out their notebooks and write down their assignment: Find out why helium balloons rise and air-filled balloons don't. I wonder if she really does know the answer to this question, but I am stopped short of finding out when Jack retrieves me for a meeting with the district superintendent.

▶ ▶ ▶

Superintendent Larry Sowder has worked in the Washington-Connors School District his entire professional career. He grew up about 70 miles north of the community, went to college nearby, and took his first teaching job in the district. He's been here 35 years, 8 of those as superintendent. He doesn't have a computer and doesn't use e-mail. This could lead you to believe he's a pretty parochial guy. You'd be wrong.

"As a coach, I had useful hard data," Larry tells me. "I depended upon it to give me information about the other team. As a superintendent, I'm data-rich but information-poor. I know a lot about who's in my schools and who's in which program. But I don't know which programs have really made a difference."

Earlier that day, I had told Jack that I'd become interested in school data. I was beginning to suspect that data about student performance, put in the hands of teachers, might be the most important thing a computer has to offer. Jack replied, "You have to talk to Larry. I think you two speak the same language."

For a long time, data had been a foreign language to me. I spoke the language of content, instruction, curriculum, books, and software programs, not data. But I was starting to develop an ear for the language of numbers about student learning.

Larry tells me about the state's educational data system. It is funded by the legislature to allow comparisons across districts in the state. "Why," Larry asks, "have we been auditing financial records but not student performance records? And don't confuse activity with accomplishment," he advises me. "We *do* a lot; we need to know what it's getting us."

The state system produces tons of data, Larry says, but not in a format that reaches down and helps the classroom teacher drive instruction. And it doesn't help Larry know which of the many initiatives he has launched in Washington-Connors make a difference.

"We have Head Start, Even Start, a pre-K program, the after-school enrichment, Saturday school, summer school, and parenting programs at the two public libraries in this district," he recounts. "We were early investors in computers, and you've seen the newest programs we're using today. They all serve a purpose, but I don't have data that tell me this initiative or that software system produces lasting effects.

"And what effect," Larry wonders aloud, "do suspensions have, or retentions? And do teachers with advanced degrees make any difference in how students perform? We can guess, but I want to know."

Several years ago, Larry began thinking about these questions. How, he wondered, could he use the data about students' families—gender, health, school performance, absentee rates, programs participated in, textbooks used, and more? How could he take these data and extract information to guide his choices? And more important to him, how could it help teachers help kids?

Larry is not a computer user, but he thought computers might hold the answer. He approached a software engineering firm in a nearby town and asked the owner, an engineer, if a computer could do this job for him. He was told that it could, but that he shouldn't try to reinvent the wheel.

The engineering firm developed a Request for Information (RFI). Larry persuaded four other districts to join him, and the company interviewed administrators and teachers from each. The RFI then went to 22 companies. It contained 131 specifications or attributes that an ideal data management system would have.

Four companies responded to the RFI. Two were interviewed, and one was selected. During purchase contract negotiations, Larry lobbied the remaining four districts in the county to enter a consortium. Over a period of several years, the winning instructional management information system will be adopted and used countywide. Will it give Larry and his fellow superintendents what they want? It is too early to tell.

The dismissal bell rings. Buses are at the front door. Jack leaves to see the students off, Larry goes back to his office down the street, and I head to an after-school enrichment class.

Viewpoint

When I think of Washington-Connors Elementary School, four words came to mind: pride, energy, data, and concern. Larry, the superintendent, set a tone of pride without a speck of complacency. It was clear that he wanted the best for his people, and he wanted to find ways of knowing what "the best" was.

His elementary school principal and teachers shared his energy and pride. The teachers were discerning about students and the materials they used with students. Cheryl Putnam depended on a reading motivation program and a reading instruction software program to help her teach and to provide data about what the students had learned. In their own ways, Cheryl, Carol Ludgate, and Anita

Parker showed me that the classroom computer is a tool for students *and* teachers.

At Washington-Connors, I noticed not a closed, two-way relationship between student and computer, but a lively, triangular relationship among student, computer, and teacher. I realized that in the schools where I had seen children sitting at computers, pecking at the keys with listlessness, it was not just that the students were unengaged with the technology, but that the teachers were unengaged, too. Computers were too often expensive electronic worksheets intended to keep some of the class occupied while teachers attended to others. The kids at computers probably figured out that the teachers didn't really care what they were doing as long as they were quiet. Eventually the students quit caring themselves. This was not the case in Washington-Connors classrooms.

Finally, I think about how Superintendent Larry Sowder hoped to use computer-generated information to shape district policy and guide his decisions. He wanted a system that could reach down into the classroom and provide useful information to his teachers. That, I have concluded, might just be what computers can do best.

5

Mitchell
Elementary School

"I'VE LISTENED AND DONE WHAT YOU TOLD ME EVERY TIME before, but not this time."

A thin, pale, 6th grade girl glares with apprehensive defiance at the school principal. Over her shoulders hangs an ill-fitting imitation black leather jacket. Her teacher sent her to the principal's office for breaking a school rule: No jackets in class. It seems that the girl is ashamed of the blouse she is wearing. She is angry with someone, but not with Principal Andy Pritchard. Andy looks at her and says quietly, "Come back to my office and we can talk."

He is barely out of sight when two police officers come in and ask for him. He returns, accompanied by Assistant Principal Lew Haskins. The police are looking for a 16-year-old 8th grade boy who was seen breaking into neighborhood cars. Andy and Lew tell the police that the suspect has not been in school for more than a month.

"Call if you see or hear about him," the officers request, and they head out.

This is how days start at Mitchell Elementary, a school serving students in pre-kindergarten through 8th grade . . . a school where, the principal comments, "I can be changing a diaper one minute and meeting with a probation officer the next."

Mitchell Elementary lies in the flats of a large, midwestern river town—home to proud Appalachians who came here for jobs that have now dwindled or moved south or offshore. There are 650 students at Mitchell this year, down from more than 700 a year ago. Yearly turnover is 40 to 45 percent. Seventy percent of the students are white Appalachian, 30 percent are black. One hundred percent qualify for free or reduced-cost lunches.

The administrative team at Mitchell includes two social workers and a psychologist. A juvenile court is housed in the building. Over 20 percent of the students qualify for special education services, so Individualized Education Plans (IEPs) must be written and reviewed for about 150 children each year.

Principal Andy Pritchard seems up to his challenging job. A former college football player, he began at Mitchell soon after graduation and moved quickly from teacher to assistant principal to principal. He must be 30, but he appears younger. At Mitchell, he needs a young man's energy.

▶ ▶ ▶

I'm visiting Mitchell Elementary to look once more at the computer-supported reading instruction program that I saw at both Harriet Tubman and Washington-Connors Elementary Schools. At those schools, the program was used in individual classrooms, but at Mitchell, it is used in two labs. I've been impressed with what I've seen of the reading program, and I wonder how it functions in a lab setting. I want an in-depth understanding of this program that seems to work, especially after having seen so much that does not.

Lew, the assistant principal, takes me upstairs to meet lab teacher Jeremy Williams. Jeremy is short, lean, and built like a runner. He has an undergraduate education degree from a local university and studies in the evenings for his master's in special education.

Jeremy oversees two labs housed in large, high-ceilinged class-rooms. One lab is for reading, the other for science and math. The labs face each other across one of Mitchell's wide corridors, and Jeremy is rapidly wearing a path between the two. He had expected an aide to oversee the new math and science lab while he concentrated on the reading lab. When 60 fewer students than expected showed up in September, Mitchell Elementary's staff was trimmed. Six aides were reassigned to other schools, and Jeremy was left to tend both classes.

The district's site-based management system allocates approximately $7,000 per student. With a $420,000 shortfall, Andy and Jeremy had to make some accommodations. They put off buying an upgraded management system for the reading program that would have allowed Jeremy to control the 22 computers in the reading lab from a single master control unit. Deferring the upgrade saved $25,000. Without it, however, he must sprint among five computers, each of which controls four to five other computers.

In the math and science lab, Jeremy controls nine computers from one master station. The school saved more money by acquiring a beta version of the program. Bugs remain, Jeremy acknowledges, but patches are coming and he has been able to implement the system a year earlier, and at lower cost, by not waiting for the refined version.

Students in pre-K through 2nd grade use the reading system. Kindergartners and 1st graders use the computers for math and science as well. Pre-K students come for 15-minute sessions, the others for 30 minutes. Each week, 200 children flow in and out of the labs, and Jeremy manages more than 300 individual sessions.

Jeremy is about to pick up a group of 1st graders for the day's first math and science lab. Nine students will remain with the classroom teacher while Jeremy escorts nine others back to the lab. Before departing, however, Jeremy has to set up each computer for an incoming reading class of 2nd graders. He exits the door at a near run just as that group arrives. The 18 children enter quietly, and each finds a computer with his or her name on the monitor.

As Jeremy guides the nine 1st graders into the math and science lab, I cross over to that room, where student names appear on all nine computers.

"Would you like to listen?" Jeremy asks. I nod, and he dashes to a nearby cupboard. Labels on the door read *User Manuals, Computer Software, Toner, Computer Speakers, Surge Supplies, Headphones, Headphone Covers, Computer Mouses,* and *Mouse Pads.* Jeremy cleans a set of headphones, plugs them into a computer, and offers them to me.

My headphones share a spliced plug with a set being used by a student named Donny. Jeremy points to a small chair beside Donny. As I slip on the headphones and sit down, a calendar appears on the screen, and a voice says, "Today is February 22. Click on a number that tells yesterday's date."

Donny moves the cursor to the 21 and clicks. A small bouquet of flowers appears, and the voice says, "Click on a number that tells tomorrow's date." Donny clicks 23, and another bouquet appears.

The voice then asks what today's weather is. Donny looks out at the gray February sky and drags a "cloudy" icon to today's date. A screen appears with four illustrated icons. "This is a free-choice window," Jeremy whispers to me, "a reward for doing well on earlier lessons."

Donny clicks on a snowflake, and immediately a video starts. It shows two young girls playing in the snow in a middle-class suburb, a stark contrast to the neighborhood in which Mitchell Elementary is located. The melody to "Morning Has Broken" plays to introduce the science lesson on the changing position of the sun. The video's very high production values and wry humor appeal to both adults and children. When it ends, Donny clicks for a repeat play, then another.

He clicks the remaining three icons in turn and views three successive videos that present science concepts through animation, sound, and interactive questions. Each addresses children while winking at the adult viewer. It seems clear that the producers had fun creating them, and Donny remains engaged.

"These are foundational concepts," Jeremy points out. "They complement our classroom science lessons. The management system allows me to order the lessons so they align with our district curriculum."

► ► ►

When the session ends, I return to the reading class. With an enrollment turnover of nearly 45 percent each year, the management of kids coming and going seems like an impossible task. But not for Jeremy. He enthusiastically demonstrates how he can quickly add or delete students' names from the management roster. Unfortunately, he must first remember which of the five computers holds a departing child's records.

Jeremy leaves the reading lab, guides another group of nine from their classroom to the math and science lab, returns, and quickly sets up for the next reading group. He watches to ensure that the five managing computers have posted the names of the arriving students. The children take their seats, except for one boy, who can't find his name. He looks plaintively at Jeremy.

"This is his first day," Jeremy says. He goes to one of the managing computers and asks the boy sitting there to wait a moment. Jeremy opens the management system and asks the new boy, "How do you spell your last name?"

The boy stands silently. He doesn't know. "It's Alton. A-L-T-O-N. Chad Alton," an adult voice offers. It's the teacher who had accompanied the new student to class.

Jeremy types quickly, and in a moment, Chad's name appears on the screen of a nearby computer. Chad sits down, and Jeremy cues orientation instructions. Within several minutes, Chad is clicking away and talking to the computer. I notice his teacher-escort smile and exit.

A little girl removes her headphones, walks over to Jeremy, and points to a boy whose head is lying on the keyboard. "It's okay. He's on his medicine," Jeremy explains, partly to the girl, partly to me. The boy is on a new anti-seizure medication that is not yet in balance. "He's been this way for two weeks," Jeremy notes.

▶ ▶ ▶

For the next two periods, I cross back and forth between the two labs. Jeremy sprints down hallways to gather new children, oversees squirming 4-year-olds, adds names, deletes names, moves the program forward when a bug is encountered, and finds places for special education students who arrive for their time with the reading program.

Because each class has an average of only 18 students, several of the lab's 22 computers normally sit unused. During one period, five 6th grade boys from the severely behaviorally disabled program use them. The boys sit quietly, absorbed in the 2nd grade reading program. There is no punching, elbowing, or acting out.

Two 8th grade girls show up for the second period. They look 16, but read at a 2nd grade level. Jeremy takes time to speak with them, as he did with the 6th grade boys, encouraging them and assuring them that they are welcome in the lab. The videos sustain their attention. I've seen so many children bored by programs reported to be the best software available; this interest is a refreshing change.

Not every child is quiet and content. One 7-year-old boy enters the class in a jittery two-step. He sits down, raises his legs, braces them against the computer table and pushes back, almost tipping over. He sits sideways on the seat, swinging his legs while lifting the headphones on and off repeatedly. He leans down and puts his head under the table. Jeremy speaks to him in a hushed tone, but the boy's fidgeting continues.

A boy with a hearing impairment comes in. I watch him put on the headphones while Jeremy explains that the boy's teacher wears a microphone and transmitter that send sound impulses directly to the boy's hearing aid. Jeremy hopes to configure the computer's sound so it also feeds directly into the hearing aid. The boy works quietly.

▶ ▶ ▶

Although I had intended to visit only these lab classes, Principal Andy Pritchard invites me to an assembly in the school auditorium. On the way, I admire the architectural touches of this classic art

nouveau building. Finely wrought aluminum lamps light the hallways, textured marble covers the walls, and doorways and transoms
show touches of the American arts and crafts era. My eye is drawn
to a window. Perched on a roof cornice is a ceramic figure of a
young girl reading a book. The soft colors of her clothes match the
gentle beauty of the statue.

As I continue on my way to the assembly, I hear raised voices.
Outside a classroom, an anxious 6th grade boy stands between his
teacher and a woman who appears to be his mother. "It's okay for
you to smack him," I hear the mother say "I'm going to when I get
him home." The boy is crying.

I enter the auditorium. On the stage are three tables with three
students at each. One table is draped in red, one in white, and one
in blue. The students wear T-shirts in matching colors. To the right
of the stage sits a teacher using a laptop to drive a computer projector. To the left is a large whiteboard with the words "Red,"
"White," and "Blue" at the top. Below are scores: 1,200 for Red, 0 for
White, and 200 for Blue. Across the top of the stage hangs a banner
that reads "Every Minute Counts."

The teams are competing in Social Studies Jeopardy to prepare
for the state proficiency tests. The computer flashes answers and
questions on the large projection screen. Contestants at the tables
press buzzers, and the audience members cheer for their favorite
teams. Teachers walk the auditorium aisles calming some too-fer-
vent supporters. They wear two-sided T-shirts that read, "Mitchell—
Make Every Minute Count" on the front and "We Aim for 'Achieving'
Status" on the back. Andy and the faculty have committed themselves to moving up a notch in the state's school ratings.

For the past three weeks, the school has put its regular curriculum (except for the computer labs) on hold. The focus has been
almost entirely on the upcoming test, and the school spent $1,500 on
test preparation books sold by the state. Andy shares with me a
report from a 3rd grade class. Nine of 18 students passed the sample
reading test, compared with just 3 last year. By test time, he expects
all 4th graders will be ready to score above the passing level.

▶ ▶ ▶

"What is it like working at Mitchell?" I ask Assistant Principal Lew Haskins as we leave the auditorium.

"This school is the only way out for most of the kids here," he tells me. Then he relates the story of his own life. At 21, he was working in an auto parts factory upriver. He was making extremely good money, far more than he makes now at 34. But he knew those jobs were disappearing. He went to school part-time and in five years earned his bachelor's degree in education. Then he moved here and took a job in a suburban system.

When the job at Mitchell opened up, he had a chance to get back with what he called "my people." The community's Appalachians are proud, he says, and they do not believe in welfare. If they can find work, they will. They would rather be back home, but there are no jobs there. Here they are on the bottom rung. A decent education is their only way out, and Lew is trying to help smooth the path for their kids to make it.

Viewpoint

I have become convinced that computer technology offers greatest support to students at the low end of the performance curve. Most of the students who attend Mitchell Elementary live at that end. The school was not without bright children, as the Jeopardy teams' quick answers illustrated. Still, a high percentage of Mitchell students were struggling and many had IEPs. Most arrived at the school door without the home support and broader experiences that children in more affluent communities enjoy.

Mitchell's decision to concentrate its technology investment on children in the pre-K and primary grades makes sense to me. These were children who had the most to make up and perhaps the most to gain. At higher grade levels, the reading instruction program served the very low achievers, as I saw with the five 6th grade boys and the two 8th grade girls who came to the lab.

This program did not work magic, and it did not work by itself. It worked because the principal understood it and supported it; because it complemented but did not replace the work of the classroom teacher; because it actively engaged all the senses; and because it was managed by a dedicated, organized, and energetic technology lab director. All these factors were critical to the equation. Remove any, and the equation just wouldn't have balanced.

PART II ◂◂◂

Commitment, Less Focus

A thin line separates the four schools I describe in this section from the highly focused and committed schools in Part I. Perhaps because all four of these schools served students from families with above average income, they felt less urgency to focus technology on very specific goals. They had the resources and leadership at school and district levels, but the efforts fell short of what I saw at St. Mary's, Harriett Tubman, Longworth, Washington-Connors, and Mitchell.

6

St. John's
High School

S⊤. JOHN'S IS A PRIVATE CATHOLIC HIGH SCHOOL SERVING about 950 boys in a large city in the Midwest. I have come to St. John's to see its technology program in action. For the past three years, the school has made laptop computers mandatory for entering freshmen. Now, every freshman, sophomore, and junior at St. John's uses his own laptop to record class notes, complete assignments, take tests, communicate with teachers, access the school network, and work on homework problems and projects. Next year, all St. John's students will have laptops.

I am met first thing by Sister Maggie Larkin, the school's technology coordinator. She tells me she came to the job because "I'd been in education a long time, and I got bored." She had been principal of a Catholic girls' school and was ready for a new challenge. St. John's technology initiative offered that.

Sister Maggie gives me an early-morning tour of the school. We visit a technology lab where every freshman takes an information systems course that introduces the tools and concepts of digital communication. During the summer, about half of the incoming freshmen take a typing and study skills course in the lab. Sister Maggie also teaches courses on Front Page and the Microsoft Office suite.

We visit the media center, where half a dozen students sit with laptops plugged into tabletop outlets and work on homework assignments before classes begin. Sister Maggie explains that students set up and pay for their home Internet connection so they can access the school's network and their teachers' Web sites.

Electronic books are available to biology, chemistry, and algebra students, but class sets of printed textbooks are also available in each of these classrooms. Sister Maggie is not a fan of electronic texts in their currently available form and believes some teachers use them only to say they use technology. She *is* a fan of a Web-based test maker that seven or eight teachers use. With it, they develop tests and administer them online, providing immediate feedback to students.

We visit the printer room and speak to the full-time aide. She oversees a high-speed, commercial-grade digital machine that generates all student printouts. When students print, the copies come out here. The aide goes through the printouts and puts them in personal file folders. While we visit, several students come in, thumb through the alphabetically arranged folders, take their copies, and leave. No other printers are available for students. A second printer is reserved for teachers.

▶ ▶ ▶

Sister Maggie escorts me to the teachers' lounge, where she leaves me with English teacher Tim Higgins. Tim invites me to join him in front of a laptop opened on a worktable. A network cable snakes down to a floor outlet. Next to us, two football coaches huddle, analyzing data from their team's first five games.

Tim teaches grammar and composition. As we speak, he opens up an electronic file folder. In it are student essays submitted online. He opens one that he has already corrected. He has appended to it his spoken and written comments. He clicks an icon, and I hear his voice advising the student to rewrite the opening sentence using the active voice. He clicks a second icon and a box pops up with a text message to the writer.

Tim explains that he has a repertoire of preset text comments that he affixes as appropriate. He customizes the taped comments to each written piece and returns the files electronically. The students can listen to Tim's advice and then rewrite.

As we listen to a taped comment, the coaches shut down and leave. St. John's Eagles are ready for their Friday night attack. Tim invites me to join him for his first class, freshman honors English.

We walk up to his second-floor classroom. The window shades are drawn, but ceiling-mounted fluorescent bulbs light the room. Student chairs are scattered somewhat irregularly around three walls. In the middle, tables are drawn together in groups of four or six. On top of them rest a half-dozen overfull backpacks. Other backpacks lie on the floor beside occupied student chairs.

I choose a seat in a far corner and watch as several more students arrive. They reach into their backpacks, pull out laptops, withdraw Internet cords from side pockets, plug them into wall outlets, and boot up. While waiting, many glance up at the whiteboard, where Tim has listed the names of six students who have completed the corrections requested on their last essays.

A student, shoulder bandaged and arm in a sling, enters just as class begins. He is an offensive end on the football team. Injured in last Friday night's game, he's out for the football season and half of the basketball season as well. He pulls behind him a backpack on wheels, using his catching, shooting, and writing hand. Fortunately, that writing hand will be available to take old-fashioned notes by hand.

The football player sits down and manages to open a notebook while Tim tells the rest of the class to e-mail him their homework essays if they've not already done so.

"So . . . what's happening next week?" Tim asks, probably for my benefit.

Groans rumble through the class. "Proficiencies," a boy next to me calls out.

"That's right, state tests," Tim replies. "Writing on Monday, reading on Tuesday."

He flicks a light switch to darken the room, then turns on a computer projector, focuses it on a screen, navigates to the Internet, and opens a state education department Web site that features a sample of the reading proficiency test. The students have navigated to the same site on their own laptops. Most sit with their backs to Tim, their screens facing him. As the interactive test review proceeds, the students suggest answers to sample questions, sometimes twisting awkwardly in their seats. Classroom logistics are not smooth. Still, Tim believes it's the only way to arrange the classroom. "I must be able to see their screens," he says. "Otherwise, they'd be drifting off to other sites."

When the test review ends, Tim turns off the projector. Students shut down their laptops, unplug their cords from the network, and take seats at the tables in the middle of the classroom. Tim has moved to an overhead projector, looking over and saying, "This is my low-tech approach. I've not yet converted this content to PowerPoint."

He then reviews samples for the state writing test, which, unlike the sample reading test, is not available online. He quizzes students on the distinctions between narrative, expository, and descriptive essays and stresses how they must read the writing prompts carefully to know what the test is after.

▶ ▶ ▶

The class ends, and the students gather their backpacks and move to their next class. I thank Tim and move to my next class as well, ancient history for sophomores. In this room, football plays are scrawled on the whiteboard and four or five teens sit around each of six tables.

The teacher, Matt Robinson, tells me that today will be a unit-opening activity on ancient Greece. Each team of students has chosen a topic: sports, government, clothing, theater, architecture, or the military. They hunch over their computers, skimming Web sites, thumbing through textbooks, and planning PowerPoint presentations.

Matt, an assistant football coach, joins me as I walk from group to group. His eyes dart from me to screens. "The challenge with 15- and 16-year-olds is keeping them on task. Instant messaging is a big problem. So is music."

Matt likes the laptops and wants to replace printed textbooks with electronic books. The online version of their current textbook would cost $50 per student. "Who is going to pay that?" he asks. He uses the online test maker for quizzes and exams because "it saves time correcting."

After 45 minutes, Matt has the students stop their work. He fires up the computer projector and, guided by a PowerPoint presentation, gives his opening lecture on ancient Greece. The presentation is a series of bullet points, "nothing fancy or glitzy," Matt had warned me earlier. "That takes too much time."

Students record notes on their laptops. One student, whose computer is temporarily at the help desk, takes notes by hand. He'll transfer them later.

At the end of the period, Matt reminds the students to post their notes to the class folder on his Web page. "I go over them to be sure they are learning how to take notes," he says. This, I think, is an interesting blend of the new and the old at work.

▶ ▶ ▶

During the next two 90-minute periods, I'm set to visit a freshman honors biology class, a junior health class, a sophomore English class, a sophomore geometry class, and the school's help desk, where students bring computers for repair or consultation.

Ted Stern, the freshman biology teacher, tells me that technology makes him and his students more efficient. He once spent two weeks on a Darwinism unit. Now he does it in four days, since students have access to so many more resources. Each student has a text on CD-ROM, but he tells me that 80 percent prefer to take notes from textbooks. For that, they use the printed set in his room.

Ted was once a technology skeptic: "When [Principal] Jim Sneider proposed that we do this a few years ago, I couldn't see how it was going to work, but it really does."

Next to Ted's classroom, Gene Roberts teaches geometry in the physics laboratory. Students sit at lab benches, their laptops plugged into outlets on the lab counters. I can see the screens; Gene can't. Some students check sports results on ESPN.com.

Last night's homework assignment incorporated the online math program St. John's uses. Told that the angles of a triangle have a ratio of 2:3:7, students were to find each angle. Gene asks how many students did the problem. All raise their hands. He then passes out a quiz sheet with the problem repeated.

"You didn't tell us we were having a quiz," several students protest.

"It's not a quiz," he says. "I'm just having you do the problem you did last evening." Gene doesn't doubt that the students did the problem—in fact, he can use the program's management system to verify that they did it—but he does doubt that they understood it.

The students take the sheets and work quietly, seriously. After 10 minutes Gene asks for answers. "Keep your papers," he says. "Let's discuss the problem."

It turns out that no one knows the answer or how to find it. Gene offers some leads and then has a student go to the board. Step by step, the class unravels the answer.

"When you're working these problems, don't just click through the hints that the program provides," Gene tells his students. "That's what you did last night. You thought you understood the solution, but the program was doing the thinking for you. That's the problem I have with it. You need to be able to do it on your own."

I move on to the health class, where the teacher lectures on weight management from a PowerPoint presentation. Half of the students have their computers on, taking notes. Half just listen.

Next is English. The teacher e-mails an essay quiz to the students. They work four to a table, but focus on their own screens. They complete their quizzes, e-mail them back to the teacher, and await an assignment. Then it comes: They have 35 minutes to write a character description, which they will discuss during the last half hour of class.

From there, I go to the help desk. It is a small office on the school's main corridor. A Dutch door is open at the top. Sitting behind it is Craig Elliott, a St. John's graduate who completed a computer science degree at a local university. He runs the help desk with support from student volunteers.

The help desk handles 30 to 35 problems a day. Most can be solved while the student waits. If a student must leave his computer, the help desk provides a loaner. The school purchased enough laptops so that about 40 spares are available.

"Our biggest problems happen when students try to load software and do it incorrectly. They want to add scanners, CD burners, or digital cameras. We also get problems when they try to install network cards or modems," Craig tells me.

Add-ons like these are allowed, but games cannot be loaded on the computers. Periodic, unannounced checks are made to be sure that no prohibited or unlicensed software is being used.

Craig also admits, "We had hardware problems the first year with cases cracking. We changed models and that went away, but we had to replace a faulty memory chip in every one of those. We changed to a third model this year and haven't had problems."

Viruses are a problem, Craig tells me. The Nimba virus spread through the system but was controlled quickly. It has been cleaned from the servers but is still on some student machines. A systematic program is underway to clean them up.

▶ ▶ ▶

I leave the help desk and find my way to the school office, waiting to meet with Principal Jim Sneider. I am interested in how his vision matches the school I've seen today. I want to ask Jim about the reasons for implementing this program and the results. I've sat in classes, walked the halls, and observed the help desk. Now I can get Jim's thoughts on his school's adventure.

And it is very much his school. Jim Sneider has been principal of St. John's for 11 years. He is a big man with big ideas, and those big ideas reverberate throughout the school.

"Close the door," he says as I enter his office. He's 6'2", with thin, curly hair, mussed at day's end. The door shuts out the sound of builders working on the school's new $1.5 million activity center.

I ask Jim about the school's path to where it is today. "Ten years ago we knew we had to change," he replies. "The kids were bored; the teachers were bored. I gathered the faculty and asked how we could learn to do new things.

"'Let's think that money is no issue,' I told the faculty. 'What would be the ideal environment?' Somebody said, 'A laptop for every student.'

"Laptops, we decided, would be our catalyst for change. It wasn't technology itself we were after, but technology as the catalyst for fundamental change. Some schools have used block scheduling as the catalyst; we were going to use laptops."

Teachers received laptops first. St. John's deferred buying new textbooks and saved the money for software and hardware. Tuition was boosted by $900, raising it to $5,800 per year. Funds were raised to rewire the 40-year-old building, and the school's college prep curriculum was modified. Teachers had to learn about networking and computer electronics, as well as new approaches to instruction. They took a fresh look at curriculum and teaching methods. Some teachers quit.

"Yes, we had attrition," Jim says. "Some faculty didn't want to go in this direction, so we parted ways. We lost some good people, but we were committed to change. Lots of people who choose teaching tend to seek safe ground, a controlled environment. When you introduce change, you create a lot of angst. To foster change, you need to take risks, spend money, and expect results to take time."

Jim explains that each laptop costs the school $600 a year, based on a three-year life expectancy. Add maintenance and repair and the true cost reaches $700 to $750. The $900 tuition increase provided some margin and was met with virtually no complaints.

"Are you leading the way?" I ask Jim. "Are you what the future will look like, or are you something apart from the mainstream?"

"No one in this city is following us," he says, leaning back and thinking. "St. Catherine's was ready to go our way, but their board pulled back, saying it was too costly."

I ask whether he has seen measurable benefits in student performance and whether anything has resulted that he'd not expected.

"It's too early to tell about measurable results," he answers. "You need to look at this using a five- or six-year time frame, maybe longer. A graduate student studied us for his master's thesis. We showed some growth, but it wasn't a deep study. It doesn't count for much.

"What I didn't expect were the student numbers. We have 950 students. We average 265 freshmen and graduate an average of 208. That dropout rate holds steady from year to year.

"A year ago we had 265 freshmen. This year we have 272 sophomores. We not only held our numbers, they actually increased. No other factor than the laptops explains this increase. In the past, kids could leave here relatively easily and slide into a program at another school. If they leave now, they lose their laptops."

Jim is cautious about making claims. He won't argue that St. John's is a model for the future, but he believes it offers glimpses of what's ahead.

Viewpoint

I understood Jim's clear vision and his caution in declaring it achieved. Based on what I saw during my visit to St. John's, the quality of execution fell into shades of gray, although those grays were often at the brighter, lighter end of the spectrum. For example, the laptop program was hobbled by a building designed for students with books, not computers. Wires ran awkwardly down walls and across floors. Students sat at the perimeters of classrooms, backs to the teacher, eyes on their screens. Laptops were balanced precariously on student chair-desk combinations, sharing the small writing surfaces with textbooks or paper. Too often, I saw a computer resting on a writing arm while the student balanced a textbook on his lap. In classrooms where all students faced the teacher, their screens were hidden and students were easily attracted to unrelated Web sites. In addition, the electronic books St. John's needs to maximize its technology investment are not yet the equivalent of printed books for many teachers and students. And electronic instructional programs, like the one used by the geometry students, are not yet proven effective learning tools.

However, I saw some obvious advantages to St. John's technology model. World history students had a wealth of research sources for their reports on Grecian life. Tim Higgins's students probably received more in-depth analyses of their English essays than they would have with traditional media, *and* Tim saved time doing his evaluations. Computer-based tests were self-correcting and provided immediate results. The help desk system appeared to be efficient and the school was not plagued by hardware or software problems. In some cases, I sensed that teachers strained to incorporate the student laptops into instruction. They were not yet essential tools but were used because students had them.

Jim said that laptops were his catalyst for change. I think Jim was the catalyst. His leadership could have changed the school even if he had chosen chalk as his tool for renewal.

Is St. John's the future? It is probably a step toward it, offering glimpses of what may come, but technologies need to be simplified, classrooms or furniture changed, and software refined in order for that future to arrive.

▶ ▶ ▶ 7

Longfellow Elementary School

"WELCOME TO SEA MEADOW" IS ALL THE SIGN SAYS. IT COULD add "An Historic New England Village" or "A Community of Trophy Homes for Rising Executives" or "A School System That Is Doing Technology Right." All these are true. But with typical New England reserve, it's just "Welcome to Sea Meadow."

And I do feel welcome as Chet Williams meets me in the parking lot of Longfellow Elementary School. Chet, Longfellow's technology coordinator, is lanky, in his mid-50s, and wearing a baggy cardigan sweater on this brisk October day. He and I spoke by phone three weeks ago, and I know already that Sea Meadow is a one-school district.

"We have 19 classrooms covering kindergarten through grade 8," Chet told me on the phone. "The classes are small, no more than 15 students per room in grades K through 4. We have a lab with 28 computers, plus 5 more in the library and between 2 and 4 in each classroom."

It is 7:30 a.m., and only four cars are in the lot. The school is quiet as we climb to the second floor. While we walk, Chet repeats that Sea Meadow is a wealthy town, the town of choice for successful executives and their families.

"I'm not one of them," Chet assures me, although he was born in Sea Meadow. Chet tells me how he served as a teacher in the Peace Corps for seven years. "But I didn't have a teaching certificate, so when I came back, I went to the state university for my teaching degree. That was in the late '70s. I wanted to teach writing, and I became involved with the process writing movement. When computers appeared in the early '80s, I realized they could be a wonderful tool for process writing. By then, I had a part-time position as an enrichment teacher here in Sea Meadow.

"Across the hall from my enrichment class was a teacher with an Apple IIe. I saw what it could do, and I wrote a grant request for 12 IIes. That was our first computer lab. We had a strong backer in a school board member who had lost his job. He lacked computer skills and discovered how hard it was finding a job without them. He wanted to be sure our kids were computer literate."

Chet goes on to tell how the computer has solved two important writing challenges. It helps kids who have a problem with cursive writing, and it makes frequent revision practical. Writing, he says, is a dynamic process of discovering what you think. Computers support that dynamism.

I ask if that support translates into better writing. Chet can't say it has, but he believes in the power of technology to change education and he brings enthusiasm to his work. That enthusiasm has sparked support from a group of area NetDay volunteers, who wired the school several years ago. A local cable television company provided a server that lets the school run Microsoft Office on Macs and PCs.

Chet's enthusiasm has sparked teacher response, too. I see this when we meet Rita Brennan, a veteran teacher who was once very skeptical about technology's role in education. "Rita was not sure how to integrate technology into her classes," Chet confides as we walk down the stairs toward Rita's classroom. "She's still looking for the best ways to use it."

When we arrive, Rita's 3rd grade students are at music. Like Chet, Rita is in her mid-50s. "I don't know how I could get by without my computer," she says. "I do everything on it, but in the classroom I don't want to sacrifice the basics. So here is what I do."

Rita describes how she searches for CD-ROMs to accompany every unit she teaches. She installs them on her four classroom computers for students to use during free time. She shows me her classroom computer center, set up against a wall: two tables, each with two computers. In front of each table are four chairs. "I like to have two children at each computer," she explains. "Then they can help each other. They bat ideas back and forth. They exchange ideas. It's like everyone is learning from one another," she explains.

"I feel I've made great strides," Rita adds. "I'm very conversant with computers now. They're a part of my life."

▶ ▶ ▶

Rita's enthusiasm is shared by Linda Scott, Longfellow's special education teacher and our next stop on the tour. "Special ed is a perfect place for technology," Linda says.

Stacked next to the computer on her cramped desk are at least 50 CD-ROMs. Linda sees me studying them and explains, "The state has a technology grant program. I wrote a proposal, and it was funded. It pays for an aide, plus all of this software. The grant runs three years and supports reading, writing, and math. We analyze the needs of each special ed student, then we target specific areas of need. We select a program to meet that need, and the aide works one-on-one with the student.

"Software is not a babysitter here," Linda says, firmly. "A lot of people turn the computer into a sitter—at school and at home. Not here. Of course, it's impossible to know 50 different programs well. How many do you know?" she asks me.

I answer that I know three well: Word, Excel, and PowerPoint. Maybe four if you count Outlook.

"See?" she says. "Try to know 50. You can't. And neither can my aide or I. So it is hard to align with kids' needs. But working one-on-one helps a lot."

Chet tells me that students in his computer labs do not use many programs. Once a week, he holds a lab session for each of the 19 classrooms, teaching computer basics like starting up, saving, shutting down, accessing the Internet, using the mouse, keyboarding, and using a word processor.

"I think that people have a misconception of what it means to have technology in the classroom," Chet says. "They see kids sitting at home alone on a computer and think that computer use in school is the same. It's not. Computer use in school is more teacher-directed. It has to be. Goals come from the teacher. The teacher leads the kids through the thinking process."

▶ ▶ ▶

Chet offers to introduce me to the principal, Mary Strickland. She is a strong supporter of the school's technology program. I am interested in finding out why.

"On a gut level, I feel like computers are a great advance," she says carefully. Mary, in her late 40s, has been principal of Longfellow Elementary for 17 years. She projects an aura of dignity and intellectual depth. She is a thoughtful woman.

Mary describes how the 8th grade did a unit on the 1930s. "They used PowerPoint to assemble and deliver presentations. On the Internet, they located sounds, pictures, and text about the period. They heard music from the jazz clubs of the day and speeches by J. Edgar Hoover. They had access to documents from the era. I really felt the kids who gave presentations knew what they were talking about."

As Mary speaks, I recall what Chet said about the teacher's role in guiding technology use. I visualize an effective teacher helping these students locate and evaluate content with the aid of technology. In other schools, I have seen teachers absorbed with the technology instead of the content. Too often I have seen artifice, not insight. This does not appear to be the case at Longfellow.

I ask Mary about funding. What other needs compete with technology for funding dollars? "This year it was a special-needs teacher," she replies. "Just before school began, a child with a severe disability transferred in, and he needed one-on-one attention. The special ed teacher cost us $60,000, which we had not planned for. I took it from Chet's technology budget, which meant canceling any plans for upgrades, new computers, or new software."

I learn that this was not the first time that other priorities superceded technology funding at Longfellow. For a stretch of four years, Chet was cut to half-time. His position and several instructional support positions were trimmed so that the school could afford to hire new primary teachers (and keep class sizes at 15 students). He went back to full-time two years ago.

Whether full-time or half-time, Chet appears to be a catalyst for effective computer use. As we walk back to his lab, he is hailed by the kindergarten teacher, who is sitting at her computer and spots us through the open classroom door. "Guess what I'm doing?" she calls out. "I'm re-laying out this worksheet. Now it is easier for the little ones to navigate."

She shows us a simple page of number recognition activities. "It was too crowded before, and the children didn't know where to draw their lines. Now it's clear," she says with obvious pride. Chet congratulates her, and we move on.

The next Longfellow teacher I meet is similarly enthusiastic. Ken Albers teaches 6th grade language arts. "I don't know what I'd do without computer technology," he says. "Let me see: I've used technology seven times already today. I e-mailed twice, printed out a copy of a test, retrieved a project from a file, created a vocabulary test, helped a student save a file, and typed out a test."

"What about using technology in your instruction?" I ask. Ken describes how he has students take notes from information they locate on the Web. Notes must be in their own words. No cutting and pasting allowed. In fact, students in Ken's class need permission to print documents, and Ken verifies that any printed material is original.

Ken shows me two class projects: autobiographies and interest magazines—both printed and bound. The autobiographies include family and school pictures, vacation photos, and other scanned memorabilia. The magazines address topics like skateboarding, soccer, cheerleading, and boy bands. The text, Ken tells me, is developed using process writing methods. Students go through repeated drafts and revisions. Ken grades on content and the student's use of media.

Has the state testing program affected the way Ken teaches or uses technology? "Not at all," he says resolutely. He still requires his students to read six assigned novels and two pleasure books per term. He has not changed his curriculum because of state tests. But then, I think, the students he teaches are not at risk of failing these tests. Classes at Longfellow are small, and the faculty is stable. Strong support services are available for students having difficulty. And home life in Sea Meadow is rich in culture and in commitment to education. Although technology funding has fluctuated, the town's support for education has never wavered.

Ken's disregard for testing is not shared by Margaret Ashmond, the school guidance counselor. Margaret has been at Longfellow for 20 years. She has seen regular change in the tests used and in attitudes toward assessment. With the passage of the No Child Left Behind legislation, she sees more change in the years ahead.

At one time, Longfellow Elementary administered the Iowa Tests of Basic Skills yearly to each student in grades 3 through 8. The administration uses the results to evaluate individual, class, and whole-school performance. "One year we saw a score drop-off on the reference skill subtests. We adjusted our instruction, and the next year our performance rebounded," Margaret tells me. For several years, the school used another test series for grades 4 though 8, experimented with portfolio evaluation, and incorporated a high school entrance test into the assessment lineup. Then the state introduced new required tests at grades 3 and 6. The smooth pattern of administering a single company's test for each grade was broken.

To guide reading placement, Margaret introduced a well-regarded reading test at the beginning of each year. She also negotiated a commitment from the publisher to report spring test results before the school year ended. These quick test results are very important to Margaret. She now looks forward to the time when computers will be used to administer tests and report results immediately.

▶ ▶ ▶

Eighth grade math teacher Kara Lashley, whom I visit next, also values immediate results. She gets them from a computer-driven math program that generates customized worksheets based on the results of a computer-scored test. It's the same program I saw at Washington-Connors (see Chapter 4).

Kara's students enter their answers onto a machine-scoreable card and feed them into a small card reader. "Kids love putting cards through the scanner and getting results right away," she tells me. "The program lets everyone move at his or her own pace. It builds confidence and challenges the best students. They get excited about it. Why? Because they get results right away," she repeats.

"Is the program expensive?" I ask.

"Yes."

"Is that a problem in Sea Meadow?"

"No."

Kara describes her other technology uses: "I do a lot of work on spreadsheets. Every time you put these 8th graders in front of a computer, they get more interested. Some are setting up spreadsheets for their family finances.

"I also do a unit on famous mathematicians. The students do research and create PowerPoint presentations. Before PowerPoint, my kids were making presentations with posters and notes written on file cards. That can't compare with PowerPoint. With all the work students put into the slides, they really get to know the content."

▶ ▶ ▶

My last class of the day is 5th grade science. Teacher Doug Melford is introducing a unit on biomes in the technology lab. Each student sits behind a computer facing the front of the room. Doug has a laptop before him and projects his screen image on a large monitor. He directs students to a Web site titled "Tour of Biomes." I had watched Chet Williams cache the site earlier in the day so Doug's

20 students could access it quickly, all at one time. Chet and Doug had planned well.

Less well-planned is the classroom seating. Doug cannot see the student screens. He guides students through the site, trying to discuss with them the implications of a climograph of Alice Springs, Australia.

"What is Alice Springs's temperature in December?" he asks. "Could Santa use his sleigh then?"

The answers are sparse. Without Doug seeing, several students have taken a shortcut on the biome site to a page called "Dinosaur Floor." There, they are playing an animated game. Doug directs attention to screen text about biomes, telling students to find information and summarize it on a worksheet distributed when class began. This is no competition for "Dinosaur Floor." Animation moves, text doesn't. Animation wins.

Viewpoint

Although the visit to the 5th grade science class showed me that not everything about Longfellow's technology was effective, quite a bit was. In some sense, this should not be a surprise. The Sea Meadow community was wealthy and involved, classes were small, and administrators and faculty had been in place for a number of years. The principal had led the school for 17 years, the guidance counselor had been there for 20. They knew the community and its kids, and still they showed enthusiasm and readiness to adapt and lead change.

Longfellow's staff did not seem like pro-technology automatons. In past funding decisions, they showed themselves willing to defer or limit technology spending in order to maintain small classes and to accommodate the needs of a severely disabled student.

At other schools, I saw occasional tension between the technology leader and classroom teachers. Most often, it occurred in schools where technology support from the principal's office was equivocal or in doubt. There was none of this tension at Longfellow. Despite Principal Mary Strickland's willingness to pare back computer staffing and investment, she always believed in technology's contribution to the school's mission. Undoubtedly, the school also benefited from having a technology coordinator with a personality that evoked response and cooperation. Chet led by anticipating staff and student needs and delivering support through service and example.

I now believe that leadership like I saw at Longfellow, St. Mary's School, Longworth High School, Washington-Connors Elementary School, and Mitchell Elementary School is essential to successful technology use. Longfellow operated under the constraints of time, space, and still-immature systems. These constraints limit technology's value in all schools, but leadership at Longfellow helped make technology a relatively valuable part of the school's program.

8

▶ ▶ ▶

Ludlow Springs
School District

THE LUDLOW SPRINGS SCHOOL DISTRICT HAS NEARLY EVERY-thing: dynamic leadership, dedicated faculty, community support, a strong tax base, plans, and purpose. All this was apparent when I visited the district's Web site. There, I could examine the district's budget, its long-range technology plan, its curriculum, links to other institutions and businesses, and many more services for teachers and the public.

There are only three schools in the Ludlow Springs School District: Ludlow Springs Elementary, Ludlow Springs Middle, and Ludlow Springs High. The number of students totals about 2,300, and the budget is $27 million—slightly less than $12,000 per student.

Fall leaves color the rolling Pennsylvania countryside as I approach the three-school campus. On my right as I enter the property is the 20-year-old high school. The elementary and middle schools are nearby, at the bottom of a sloping hill. They are three years old and were consolidated from three buildings in Milfordville, a town of 5,000 that once formed the core of the Ludlow Springs district. Expensive suburbs have cascaded from an urban area to the north, changing the demographics of the district.

Margaret Barrett, the elementary school principal, is out today. I'm met instead by Monica Baker, the technology coordinator.

"A friend of mine didn't want the job when she was offered it three years ago. She recommended me, so here I am," Monica tells me as we walk to the computer lab. She details the school's technology. Her lab has 31 computers, a black-and-white printer and a color printer, a digital camera, a computer projector, a cable television, and an interactive electronic whiteboard. Every classroom has five computers, a digital camera, a black-and-white printer, and a large-screen monitor. The media center has another 26 computers. A video production studio is on the drawing board.

The equipment has been purchased almost entirely from district funds. Because the state funding formula favors low-income districts, Ludlow Springs receives relatively little from that source. Federal funding represents only $126,000 of the district's budget.

Monica tells me that she chairs the school's technology council, which consists of representatives from each grade and from the special education staff. Monica also sits on the district technology council with coordinators from the other two schools, several administrators, and a school board member.

"Our technology plan covers administration and instruction," Monica explains. "We're looking at ways for administrators to examine quarterly grades so they can track performance and change instruction if necessary. I'm teaching Excel so teachers can enter quarterly grades on the computer and make charts that track performance visually. I'm also training special ed teachers to develop and update Individualized Education Plans on the computer."

At Ludlow Springs, they are interested in using technology to support test performance. Last year's state test scores showed a need for improvement in the area of problem solving. So Monica searched for and found a software program designed to develop problem-solving skills. However, like many efforts I will see today, there are no effective ways to measure whether this program has made a difference.

Monica views the lab as a training ground for the use of computers in the classroom. Teachers come to the lab voluntarily, signing up through an online scheduling program. Monica provides additional one-on-one instruction to teachers, some of whom also take online technology training courses. The courses, run by a California company, are very practical, she says.

"Teachers learn things they can use right away in science, social studies, or language arts. After an online lesson, they say, 'Wow, I can do that.' We're planning to start a program later this year that requires teachers to take an online assessment of their tech skills," Monica tells me as we pause momentarily at the lab door. "They'll be assigned courseware to learn and will be given a pre- and post-test."

► ► ►

In the lab, class is just getting underway. Ellen Foster, a 4th grade teacher, is introducing her science class to the Encarta encyclopedia software program. The class is working on a mammal unit, and Ellen wants students to research a mammal of their choice. She is assisted by Shannon Wright, a full-time technology aide.

The lab's computer projector hangs down from the ceiling. A dulled image of the program's interface is cast on a cream-colored cement block wall. Desks are arranged theater style. Ellen describes the rudiments of navigation, guides students to the search screen, and instructs them to type the name of an animal. She demonstrates finding the entries for polar bear, zebra, tiger, penguin, and elephant. Each student then begins an individual search.

I stroll quietly behind several chair rows and watch as students peer at their screens. Most wear headphones so that they can listen to narrated video clips. They seem inattentive to the text, and most ignore the photocopied sheet of research questions that the teacher has prepared. They click icons that promise graphics and movement, pause briefly at text and static pictures, and then click on.

Beside each computer is a small stuffed bear. One boy, lost in the labyrinthine navigation, places the bear on top of his monitor. Ellen comes over and helps him find his way back to "alligator." A page of text appears, and he clicks forward in search of an alligator that moves.

The stuffed bears, Monica explains, have dual roles. Placed on top of the monitor, the bears signal that the student has a problem; it's a way for them to get teacher assistance without calling out or hand waving. Students can also use the bears' cloth bodies to dust the monitor screens.

This encyclopedia search is the first step in creating PowerPoint presentations for an upcoming parents' night. Earlier, when Monica and I walked to the lab, I had seen walls heavily decorated with student work. Many contained photos of the students taken with the classroom digital cameras. "These are from parents' night earlier this week," Monica had noted.

I am impressed with Monica's organization and Ludlow Springs's strategic planning and practical implementation. I am puzzled, however, when Monica tells me that she is not part of the selection committee now in talks to select a new mathematics program. Such programs contain software and online activities that support instruction, but Monica has no review role in the program selection process.

Her focus is on nurturing technology skills rather than directly teaching content. She is concerned with supporting implementation of the district's K–5 technology objectives. Technology objectives for grades 6–8 are the responsibility of Claire Davies, the middle school technology coordinator, whom I will visit next.

▶ ▶ ▶

Before going to the middle school, I take a break in the teachers' lounge. I have found lounges to be good spots for learning about teachers' views on technology and other matters. Maria Bentley, a 5th grade teacher, sits at a laptop surrounded by an open textbook, several paperbound math activity books, and a copy of the state math curriculum guide. She glances from one to another, makes a keyboard entry, grimaces, looks my way, and then wonders aloud who I am and why I am here.

I tell her my purpose, and she quickly accepts a willing ear. Maria has taught for 10 years, and she is tired. She tells me that she spends three hours a night on school-related work and still doesn't get everything done. She is using this planning period to prepare a district-required quarterly assessment that 5th grade students must take. Their scores are reported to the district. Maria's earlier grimace reflected problems she was having entering and aligning math characters on the test.

Students aren't the only ones tested on math. Ludlow School District requires its elementary, middle, and high school teachers to take a math test based on the content of the student curriculum. This makes sense to Maria, but she feels heavily burdened by the pressures of time. It's a theme I've heard repeatedly from teachers. For many, time is the prism thorough which they view all their job responsibilities.

▶ ▶ ▶

I leave the lounge to meet up with Monica, and she takes me to the middle school. We pass through a large, well-lighted media center. Half of it serves the elementary school and half serves the middle school, connecting the classroom sections of each.

Claire Davies, the middle school technology coordinator, meets me at the lab door. She has 30 stationary computers plus two recently purchased carts with 20 wireless computers on them. Claire has been charged with measuring the impact of the wireless computers on student performance. She is uncertain how to start.

Everyone, she tells me, is concerned about state tests. "They are high stakes, scary," she says, and mentions that a nearby urban district was taken over by the state because of failing test scores. Ludlow Springs is in little danger of a state takeover, but the district is concerned about continually improving test performance.

"Evaluation is a problem we have here," Claire acknowledges. "We immerse kids in technology, but the missing piece is, how do we know that kids are learning? I help teachers develop rubrics to evaluate, but we don't have hard numbers."

Claire says that she focuses on building productivity skills. In college, she took some programming courses and became very comfortable with computers. Upon graduation, she substitute-taught in the district, and then took a job in industry, where she became well acquainted with productivity software. When the district invested in computers, they invited Claire to teach the use of productivity tools. She also teaches Internet skills.

"I encourage teachers to use technology and the Internet at teachable moments," she says. "For example, an earth science class was doing a unit on volcanoes when a Mexican volcano erupted. I helped the teacher put together a volcano Web quest. As a result, students discovered lots about volcanoes in Mexico and elsewhere."

Claire encourages me to look into some classrooms to see how technology is being used. Teachers know I'm visiting today, so I can enter and exit classes easily. From the door of a social studies classroom, I see the word "covenant" projected on a screen. The teacher controls the projector from his laptop, asking the class to use the word in a sentence. He advises them not to define the word in their sentence. After several unsuccessful tries, he gets a response that satisfies him. "Covenant" fades out and "bazaar" appears.

Across the hall, a language arts teacher projects a page of text with several footnotes. I squint to read the projected text, confident that it's legible to students' eyes. The class is studying style guidelines for a research paper. The teacher reviews several bibliographical formats, projecting and discussing them articulately with the students, who seem to be similarly articulate.

▶ ▶ ▶

The class bell ends the discussion, and I return to the computer lab. This period accommodates band, chorus, and other activities. Students can also take a study hall or work on assignments in the computer lab. Half the seats are filled when I get to the lab.

I walk around and observe. A girl fills in an electronic activity sheet for her German class. The fingers of another student fly on the keyboard as she types a social studies report. One girl fills in a fitness profile for her health class. Two boys watch animated videos from the Encarta encyclopedia. One boy, working on a social studies assignment, asks Claire, "Is Rome in Italy?" and then, "Do Italian people come from Italy?" Another works on a spelling program. A girl comes in from a cooking class, worrying aloud that she smells like the chicken stir-fry she just made.

Claire strolls over to join me and comments that 75 percent of the school's teachers use technology regularly. Sixty percent of these use it a lot. That 60 percent would probably agree that technology helps their students learn better.

Young teachers, Claire says, don't know how to integrate technology into the curriculum. Teachers with 25 to 30 years' experience often resist, and then embrace it. I've observed this pattern elsewhere, and I think about it as I find my way to the high school, where I've generally found the most experienced teachers. Will these teachers fit the profile: initially resistant to technology, but enthusiastic and effective once converted?

▶ ▶ ▶

At the high school, I meet Technology Coordinator Marvin Justice. Marvin is an experienced teacher and an early adopter. He started using Radio Shack TRS-80s more than 20 years ago. He then used Apples, until the school board adopted PCs because they had become the standard in business. In Ludlow Springs, only the music department still uses Macs.

As we walk through the halls, I hear videos playing in two social studies classrooms. Marvin says he looks forward to the day when all videos will be digitized so that teachers can download them in the classroom and show them on a large-screen television or with a computer projector.

We pass a classroom where keyboarding is being taught. This is one of the school's four business labs. Each contains 30 computers. Marvin tells me these labs are busy all the time. Every 9th grader must take a keyboarding and word processing class, and every 10th grader takes a spreadsheets and databases class. The language lab has 29 computers; the library has 26. Classrooms have anywhere from two to six. All this technology costs money, but Marvin confirms that money has not been a constraint in the district.

"We do a lot of work up front," Marvin says, "so by the time budget decisions are made, we can defend them well. We always present budgets as three-year plans. That spreads out the cost. The language department wanted to buy and install a new lab all in one year. To do that, we'd have to cut a lot of spending in other areas, so we spread the purchase over three years to be sure other projects could keep moving forward.

"We also run all technology budgets before the board member who sits on our tech committee. He's a good bellwether. The board wants technology to drive higher test scores. One way to do that is to use the computer to analyze performance and then adjust the curriculum on the basis of the analyses," Marvin continues.

I ask him about the issues he faces as technology coordinator. Getting software on time is one. The district creates its budget in July, so new software cannot be ordered until after that, and products often do not arrive in time to be mounted on servers and available for use until some time after the new school year starts. At the elementary level, that's not a problem, Marvin says, but the middle school teachers want their new software programs within two weeks of school opening, and high school teachers want theirs on the first day.

If this type of delay is common elsewhere, what does it say about the importance of computer use? Are computers an optional luxury at the elementary level, important but not critical for middle schools, and essential when computers are used for instruction within a high school course? Just what do computers mean to how schools work?

Viewpoint

Computers were supposed to transform schools. But so were videodiscs, television, and radio. Thomas Edison predicted that motion pictures would make teachers unnecessary. Before that, blackboards and wax slates were probably hailed as revolutionary tools. And slowly, those earlier technological innovations *did* change some instructional practices.

Computers may nudge schools toward change as well, but I'm inclined to believe that change will be evolutionary, not revolutionary. Ludlow Springs schools, like similarly affluent Longfellow Elementary (see Chapter 7), organized and implemented its technology plan well. The three schools in the Ludlow Springs district had virtually every technology tool, full-time technology coordinators, strong administrators, trained teachers, and an involved school board.

The tools were new, but the methodologies they used were not. For example, I saw 4th graders researching science reports much like 4th graders have always done, but with a digital encyclopedia, not a print volume from the library. I saw middle schoolers studying vocabulary, but the words were projected from a computer display, not from an overhead projector.

In all three Ludlow Springs schools, the teaching that I observed did not seem to follow the constructivist model that shapes so much of the technology vision. That may be a blessing or a disappointment, depending upon where you stand on constructivism. Still, if you had been standing next to me during my visits to these schools, seeing what I saw, you would have seen a teacher here or there who assumed a changed role in the classroom, who tried to facilitate student learning rather than direct it. When these efforts were successful, students were active and engaged; when these efforts were unsuccessful, students seemed to be going through the motions only to satisfy the teacher.

Unquestionably, technology does offer tools that can improve what people do and how they do it. For most of us, a spreadsheet is better than a pencil and column of figures or a calculator. We execute bigger calculations more quickly with a spreadsheet. But we also make bigger mistakes more quickly. Computers and spreadsheets have transformed the way we do business; in the end, however, a business still has to take in more than it spends. The spreadsheet does not change the basic rules. Similarly, computers are new tools for schools, but they are unlikely to transform schools into radically different institutions. The fundamental rules are likely to remain the same.

"Transform" is a value-laden term, implicitly suggesting movement toward something better. What is better depends on what we think is good and what we think is bad. So I say the following, knowing the ambiguity and latent controversy that "transform" carries with it: I believe that computers, as they now exist and are used, will not transform schools and will not have measurable effects on performance. There are too few computers, they are given too little time and space, and they are too costly and complex. That said, I believe they can in the relatively near term have a transformative effect on small numbers of students and upon some narrow but very important school activities. Their long-term potential to transform will depend upon technological advances in miniaturization, in wireless communication, and in memory systems, as well as other advances we can't yet imagine.

▶ ▶ ▶ $\mathcal{9}$

Western Hills
School District

AT WESTERN HILLS SCHOOL DISTRICT, A SUBURBAN SOUTHERN
California district of 32,000 students, I am introduced to a school
and a dream. The school is Sagebrush Middle School; the dream is
a new high school that is a year away from opening.

Western Hills is a blue ribbon system. When organizing my
study, I intended to focus primarily on low-profile systems. No one
could call Western Hills low profile. The district is nationally recognized for its technology planning and implementation. I have come
here because of my growing interest in data systems that support
instruction. My first order of business is to attend a meeting at the
district administrative office.

"We're replacing our current data system," says Lance Curtin, the
district database manager, as we sit in his crowded office peering at
an oversized monitor. Blue, red, and green data cells stand out on
a complex spreadsheet. "We've configured this to highlight essential
data," he explains. "We are in trial mode now. This data's not live,
but archived from past years."

Lance goes on to tell me that Western Hills has grown unhappy with the pioneering, regionally developed data system they have been using. Online response time is very sluggish, and users are discouraged by the amount of time it takes to process a query. The system we're looking at was developed by a national leader in data mining. It analyzes, correlates, and reports on relationships among data pulled from multiple sources, including test scores, student personnel records, demographic data, and attendance records. The district's goal is to have data help answer two key questions: "What is working?" and "What needs to be fixed?"

I ask Lance if the system requires teachers to input a lot of data. He thinks not, because each elementary school has a staff person assigned to assemble and enter data. Lance explains that he is working to build a system that will save time, not take it. (I will think of this comment later in the day, when a skeptical teacher comments, "When technology saves me time, *then* come see me.")

Lance and I are joined by Paul Simson, the district technology coordinator. Paul is a bigger-than-life person, both in the small office where we meet and in the larger world of public education. He has shaped the national reputation of Western Hills's technology program.

"Inequity is not having a champion," Paul notes, as we discuss how he ensures that district schools benefit equally from technology. Some elementary and middle schools, he tells me, give a free period each day to a teacher who supports technology integration and use. These schools are better off than those without a designated champion.

Unlike many districts I have visited, none of Western Hills's elementary or middle schools have full-time technology coordinators. Few of the elementary schools have computer labs. When California implemented class-size reduction, the district dismantled its elementary school labs and converted the space into regular classrooms. One solution being tested is wider use of mobile wireless systems, which can turn any classroom into a computer lab. Some of these systems have been bought with donations from industry. Paul and his staff have established a number of partnerships with area businesses. Most district schools also have technology foundations that accept tax-deductible contributions.

Paul explains that the foundation money is critically important. Family incomes are high in Western Hills, but per-pupil spending is $2,000 lower per year than in a nearby urban district.

I ask for and get a few more details about technology in the district. Paul's office provides the schools with a wide area network, mobile television services, video conferencing, curriculum guidelines, and the centralized data system. The schools then choose which technology they will use and how they will support it. Paul also chairs the district's technology advisory committee.

"What competes with technology for funding?" I ask Paul.

"Mostly personnel," he replies. "Some people know how to use people better than technology."

► ► ►

Paul wants me to visit a school that he thinks uses both well: Sagebrush Middle School. It's just 10 minutes away, located in a canyon area of new, high-income, single-family homes. When I arrive, I'm met by Principal Regina Greene.

Sagebrush has 1,500 students, Regina explains. Student turnover is less than 10 percent a year. In her four years as principal, she has seen fewer than five teachers leave the school. Today's faculty includes 78 full-time teachers.

The student population is diverse. About 10 percent of Sagebrush's students are of Philippine descent, 7 percent are Chinese, 11 percent are from other Asian backgrounds, 9 percent are Hispanic, 2 percent are black, 2 percent are Middle Eastern, and the balance (59 percent) are white or unspecified in the statistics. These demographics suggest the atypical character of Sagebrush.

As is the norm for the district, the school has no full-time technology coordinator. That role is handled part-time by Justin Baker, a science teacher. Each classroom teacher has a computer and a large-screen presentation monitor. There is a large computer lab and another half that size, plus a math lab, 10 computers in the media center, and a 4-computer mini-lab for physical education and health.

I ask Regina whether she feels computers have a measurable effect on student performance. "They probably don't have a direct effect on our SAT 9 scores," she replies, "but technology keeps students engaged. If you pulled technology from Sagebrush, our SAT 9 scores would fall because students would be less engaged. Technology classes allow kids to be the drivers. *That's* how technology helps test performance."

Sagebrush has also tried to increase test performance through curriculum reform. For example, I learn that the school has combined applied chemistry and art classes to inject more test-relevant content into the art course. When we visit an art class, the teacher is introducing a unit on the periodic table. The students are to create graphic presentations of a chemical element using computers and traditional art media.

Next, Regina and I visit a combined physics and technology class. Two teachers stand at the front of the room, handling the class in tandem. At the back of the room is a physics lab with computer stations and a variety of lab instruments and materials for use in physical science demonstrations and experiments.

Classes in the humanities strand are also combined. Language arts and social studies are taught in a three-period block. However, because social studies content is not covered by the state tests, language arts tends to get greater attention in this combined class. This year, the language arts teachers are emphasizing writing to the prompts that students will encounter in the essay portion of the SAT 9 test.

As we leave the physics lab and head for the chemistry classroom, I ask Regina about other uses of technology at Sagebrush. "We use computers with our LD [learning disabled] students, too," she replies. "We have a class of 12 taught by our LD teacher and two aides. We also have a class of students with multiple disabilities, who are taught on a one-to-one basis. In all of these classes we use computers or computer-based assistive devices.

"In addition," she continues, "we have a special sound system for students with impaired hearing. The teacher has a wireless mike, and there are special speakers in the room. The system moves with the child who has the hearing impairment, but once a teacher gets used to it, she wants to keep it for use with nondisabled students, even when the hearing-impaired student moves on."

Regina and I walk toward the chemistry classroom. The teacher, Jennifer Carroll, is meeting for the first time with this group of students, who will take chemistry during third period this week and art-related classes during third period next week. When we enter the room, Jennifer is introducing herself. She shows a PowerPoint presentation about herself and her class on the television monitor, then opens a Web page. It describes the content and requirements of the class and is accessible by students and parents at any time.

On the way back to the office, Regina mentions that all teachers at Sagebrush use computerized grade books. "Once they learn it, they save time. The grades they enter into it are posted directly to their Web sites. Of course, only the student or his or her parents can see them."

Regina models software use for her staff. She uses her laptop when she does classroom observations. She keeps her calendar on a handheld computer. She communicates with parents by e-mail. All of these save her time. I don't think she would use them if they didn't.

▶ ▶ ▶

I say goodbye to Regina and Sagebrush and head to what I've been told is the future of education in the Western Hills district: Sunset Hills High School, still on the drawing board and set to open next year. I have a meeting scheduled with the new school's principal and planning team; I am especially interested in how the principal expects to use the district's new data system.

In the temporary office occupied by the Sunset Hills team, two men sit at desks in the center of the room. Each is on the phone. A woman sits at a desk off to the side. As I walk toward her, I see that the walls are covered with architect's drawings, detailed flow charts, and handwritten sheets that seem to deal with curriculum planning.

Before I reach the woman's desk, the younger of the two men completes his call, stands up, extends a hand to me, and says, "I'm Thad Wilton. I'm the English department member of the planning team. You're here to talk about technology, aren't you? Then you need to talk with Pete Adams." He nods toward the other man, still on the telephone. "I'm not into technology too much," he adds.

Pete finishes his call, comes over, and welcomes me. He also introduces me to the office's female occupant, Kerry Mullins, who is the librarian/media center member of the team. Pete explains that he has been working on the Sunset Hills plan for three years. Before taking this planning job, he was the principal of another district high school. "We come here with a history," he tells me, implying that the plan for Sunset Hills will be based upon the experiences of the team members. "Technology will be a service to what we do in the school, not an add-on. We are being careful not to embrace technology for technology's sake. For example, we're not putting a computer projector in every classroom. Many of them would just sit unused. Instead, we'll install computer projectors where they will get use. Also, we were getting pressure to put in an expensive video streaming system. Yes, it's the latest technology, but it requires teachers to order videos from a central station. The planning team felt that was overkill that didn't really benefit the teacher. We're not going in directions that don't serve teachers.

"We have a customer-service orientation," Pete continues, pointing out that the team's administrative coordinator came from a technology company where she was a customer service administrator. "We want our technology to supply teachers with timely information about student performance. Sunset Hills will operate on data-based decisions. Our systems have to supply teachers with the data they need."

Pete then explains that the Sunset Hills plan follows guidelines published by the National Association of Secondary School Principals and the state of California. These guidelines emphasize smaller learning communities, interdisciplinary teams, and efficient use of time. He walks over to an architect's drawing of the campus and shows me how the school will be divided into areas. The areas have two buildings with 20 classrooms each. The campus is circular, with the areas radiating out from administrative buildings in the center. At the outer parameter are pads for mobile classrooms, should enrollment go beyond the planned 2,100.

"The classroom is our prime administrative unit," Pete says. "Each classroom teacher will be assigned 20 students. He or she will advise those students for four years. We won't have a separate large counseling staff. After all, counselors are information resources and information disseminators. Teachers and technology can do that."

Pete strolls over to Kerry Mullins's desk. He and Kerry show me an artist's rendering of Sunset Hills's media center. It looks like a futurist's idea for a Starbucks coffee shop. An expanse of glass looks out on surrounding hills and students sit reading at tables and on couches. Some have wireless laptops before them.

"We are planning our library services in collaboration with the curriculum teams," Kerry says. "As educators, we have to build information literacy, and I need to integrate library functions into subject areas. We will place a major emphasis on literacy."

Pete elaborates, "Reading is accessing information. Students have to learn to read in order to access information. Right now students don't read. Textbooks are dumbed down, and we develop lessons that make reading unnecessary. With our plan, we'll all become teachers of reading."

Sunset Hills's academic curriculum is to be divided into four areas: language arts/social studies; math/science; fine and performing arts; and international business. Each area will have co-leaders, one responsible for administration, the other for curriculum. The curriculum will be organized so teachers will have an average of 105 students each term, rather than the customary 165.

"Our academic standards will be based on the new California exit exams," Pete says. "Collaborative teams at the district level will be charged with developing common assessments for each curricular area. They'll be administered three times a term, and all students will take the same assessments. That should give us predictive information on how they'll perform on the exit tests.

"The technology system has to drive information to the teacher on how each of their 20 kids performs. It has to give information to the curriculum teams so they can make decisions on how the curriculum should be modified. We won't just be pushing data out. Every subsystem will have built-in data feedback loops, so that information goes two ways."

Sunset Hills's construction budget is $48 million. Technology accounts for $2.3 million of that, or slightly less than 5 percent. As I leave the office at the end of the afternoon, Pete points to a patch of land high on a hill, about a half-mile to the west. Construction trucks move in and out around partially completed buildings. That's Sunset Hills, he tells me.

I know I want to visit Sunset Hills when the school is open. How will the dream turn out? How will the reality compare to the vision?

Viewpoint

I'm not naïve. Neither am I cynical, usually. I believe parts of the Sunset Hills vision will be realized. There is, I know, a thin line between vision and hallucination, but what I saw at Sunset Hills falls solidly on the side of vision. The interdisciplinary teams may not work together perfectly; the teacher/counselor role may need to be modified; the customer service mantra may be edged out by a more traditional call for placing a larger monkey on the student's back; and accumulating, disseminating, analyzing, and acting upon data may be more expensive and complicated than the vision allows. In the end, I expect that students will be well served, teachers will engage, and good decisions will be shaped by data more often than in the past.

My cautious optimism springs from what I saw at the Western Hills central office. District leaders were installing a robust system. It seemed that they had learned from past missteps and were working to anticipate teachers' problems—for example, by providing help for data entry. The district leaders saw themselves as supports for teachers and building-level administrators, not as their adversaries. Although the administrators at Western Hills had visionary ideas, they also had a foot solidly planted where teachers live: a world where time is short and information thin. Because they showed that they understood the real world of the classroom, I believe their plans just might work.

PART III ◄◄◄

Hit-or-Miss Commitment

I sought out average schools, and the schools I present in Chapters 10 thorough 16 meet that designation. Of course, they are average only in their use of technology; on many other measures, they may exceed that classification. In fairness, City Academy (see Chapter 13) might have rated an above average computer-use designation, had it not been troubled by a transient technology problem when I visited. The other six schools in this section were marked by a lack of focus and a haphazard commitment on the part of faculty and administration. These visits were very important in shaping my conclusions and recommendations because they seem the most representative of schools across the nation.

▶▶▶ 10

Springdale
High School

I PULL INTO THE PARKING LOT OF SPRINGDALE HIGH SCHOOL
on a hot June day. Springdale is a comprehensive high school
located in an upper-income suburb of a midsized Ohio city. The
2,400 students are organized into four administrative units that provide a small-school feel in a big-school environment.

Maggie Lewis, Springdale's technology coordinator, meets me at
the office, and we walk back to the computer lab. It is empty except
for two middle-aged male teachers who huddle at a computer in one
corner. They are deep in discussion and are not disturbed by Maggie and me. We begin a conversation of our own, and I learn that
Maggie was a hospital nurse until age 35. She then switched careers,
returning to school to become a special education teacher. Her
approach to education is based on the medical model: lots of practical, hands-on experience built on real-life problems and projects.

Maggie is a self-taught computer user, first working with an
Apple IIe that she rolled on a cart from class to class. As a special
ed teacher in the high school, she taught the higher-functioning

developmentally disabled students to use spreadsheets for payroll, inventory and production record keeping—skills they used in jobs acquired through Eagle Enterprises, a services company that placed developmentally disabled students with local companies.

In 1998, Maggie became Springdale High School's technology coordinator. The state of Ohio was then implementing SchoolNet, a $600 million initiative to wire schools and put computers into class-rooms. "They flooded the district with computers," Maggie tells me, "but they put the cart before the horse. We had plenty of comput-ers, but we didn't have teachers who were ready to use them or an administration committed to technology."

She also worries that new teachers, whom conventional wisdom expects to lead the technological revolution, may be tepid advo-cates. "They are coming to us with a direct-instruction orientation because that is how they were taught at schools of education," she says. It's unsettling to this proponent of project-based learning.

Springdale has four labs: a writing lab for the English depart-ment, a graphics lab, a math lab, and a business studies lab. Each of these labs has 30 computers. One special-purpose classroom has a videoconferencing system. In every classroom, the teacher has a computer workstation attached to a 34-inch television monitor.

"Our technology program could be much stronger than it is," Maggie contends. "We virtually ignored training. In the summer of 1998, when the computers were being installed, teachers were given a day's training on very basic things: how to log on, how to save to the network, how to access the Internet, how to use e-mail. There was no requirement and no urging from the administration to inte-grate technology into instruction."

Computers aren't Springdale's only technology. First-year sci-ence, Maggie explains, is taught with a laser disc system. "Students work in groups of three or four with the laser disc program and without a textbook. The students are very engaged and test scores have skyrocketed since the program started."

Although every teacher at Springdale has a classroom computer, e-mail use is optional. So is any further computer training. Twice each year, the district holds inservice workshops, during which teachers take 14 hours of classes. Teachers can choose technology classes during this time, but they don't have to.

"We've had our successes," Maggie says. "See those two men there? One is the basketball coach. He and the other teacher of at-risk students were real technophobes two years ago. Last year, they took part in a training program sponsored by the university. They learned how to use technology for project-based learning. They had to use technology to build a legal case for allowing an activity called base jumping in national forests. That hooked them, and this year they developed their own technology-based course. Their students used the Internet for research and used a graphic organizer program to guide discussion about the problem of students at malls. Then they used the graphics lab to develop a brochure to hand out at the mall. The kids learned and so did the teachers."

► ► ►

Maggie then takes me to the videoconferencing classroom. Springdale is part of a consortium with three other suburban districts. Each has created online courses that incorporate videoconferencing segments.

"We have integrated videoconferencing and online computer instruction," Maggie says. "Last year we purchased some online courses for our students, but only 8 of the 30 students who signed up completed them. These were bright students, but high school kids want to know their teacher. They found the online courses too impersonal. By combining online and TV, the students can have visual contact with the teachers."

Videoconferencing with off-campus experts has been more successful. Maggie explains: "A class of business students has interviewed the corporate marketing manager of a company in North Carolina. And a physics class asked the question, 'Why do we have to know physics?' of a physicist from an aviation lab."

I ask Maggie what policies she would set if she controlled the school's technology agenda. First, she says, she would require that all teachers participate in technology training. Problem-based instruction would be promoted and straight lecturing discouraged. She would institute block scheduling to allow more time for projects and invest in mobile carts with wireless laptops. These carts would be rolled to a teacher's room and the laptops distributed to the students. Finally, the technology staff would be part of curriculum writing. To Maggie's chagrin, a recently developed math curriculum was published without the inclusion of tech components, and no representative from the technology staff served on the writing committee.

Viewpoint

Unfortunately, my year-end visit to Springdale coincided with exam day, so it was not practical to go into classrooms. I did, however, walk the halls with Technology Coordinator Maggie Lewis, eat lunch in the school cafeteria, and chat with teachers while eating.

As I visited schools in the following months, I picked up echoes of my Springdale visit. For one thing, Maggie, like many other technology coordinators, was a strong proponent of a project-based, constructivist-inspired approach to learning. For another, Springdale's classroom technology set-up—the computer workstation with the 34-inch monitor—was very typical. Finally, I saw evidence that a successful technology program needs more than wired buildings and powerful computers. Springdale began with the naïve assumption that wires and hardware were the starting points: "Install the technology and they will come." Apparently, this was a widespread dream in districts around the country. The reality, I learned, was quite different.

► ► ► # 11

Harrison Elementary School

IT'S EARLY AUGUST AND I'M DRIVING THROUGH CALIFORNIA'S Imperial Valley. Once exclusively agricultural, it is now dotted with the bedroom communities of Bay Area commuters. Back in June, I located several California districts with year-round calendars. Four e-mails and several phone calls put me in touch with Bruce Conrad, the technology coordinator at Harrison Elementary School, a middle-to-upper-middle class school in an eight-building district at the edge of the Imperial Valley.

I drive by newly built shopping centers anchored by 12-pump 7-Elevens and Safeway supermarkets and bordered by a succession of subdivisions with names like Sussex Acres, Brittany Estates, and Hampshire Villas. On a street of near-trophy-sized homes, I see a sign for Harrison Elementary School.

This instant neighborhood is served by an instant school. Harrison has 36 classrooms, all portable, anchored around a fixed-construction administration center. In the office, I'm told that Bruce is expecting me in the computer lab. As I exit the administrative building, I discover a collection of ramp-served portables arranged in pods of four to six classrooms. These are separated by spacious playgrounds and a lunch area, covered, but without sides.

On the ramp outside of the lab are a couple dozen backpacks, some with Razor scooters, helmets, and kneepads attached. I step around the schoolbags and into the lab. Bruce calls out a hello. "I'm just starting a 4th grade social studies activity," he says. "Take a seat and I'll get going."

I slip into a chair at the back of the room. I see the backs of 29 heads looking at 29 iMac screens. Facing the class, Bruce begins the lesson. On the other side of the room, also in the back, is the regular 4th grade teacher, Connie Burns.

An image of a desktop, cast by a projector hanging from the ceiling, appears on the screen to Bruce's left. With a few mouse clicks, Bruce brings up an outline map of California. Today's activity is to type sentences about California's regions, then cut and paste them onto the map. Bruce tells the students to find the map file they saved from last week's class. Several hands shoot up. Manny wasn't here last week. Brandon can't find his file. Christa wasn't here either. Kenneth didn't bring his activity sheet.

Bruce tells Brandon to wait and then walks around and checks the other 28 computers. He pauses with several students, asking them questions about file names and folder locations. Brandon says he can't do anything because his file disappeared. Bruce tells him to be patient. Brandon can't. Bruce reaches Brandon, executes the find function, and locates the file inside another student's folder.

With the maps launched on each computer, the students open Word and type in sentences. Connie, the classroom teacher, had assigned them to write sentences on an activity sheet using information found in their social studies textbook. "What should we type about the coast?" Bruce asks. He coaxes answers: "lots of large cities"; "sunny and sandy in the south"; "rocky cliffs in the north."

As Bruce leads the discussion of regional characteristics, half the students are engaged, but the other half are distracted, opening files on their computers, talking with one another, or looking dreamily out the window at the cloudless blue sky. Connie tells them to pay attention.

The students type out descriptions. Several are touch-typing, but most hunt and peck laboriously, a letter at a time. Hands shoot up as one student after another has a problem with cutting and pasting the text box. Bruce moves from student to student, discussing what the problem might be and what solutions might be tried. As he works with one student, others express frustration or boredom.

One boy, who has paid little attention to Bruce, is at a loss as to what to do. Connie takes the mouse, activates a drop-down menu, executes the find function, locates the boy's map, cuts and pastes the sentences, and returns to the back of the room.

Is this the exciting new world of computer education? Bruce is no novice as a teacher, computer user, and educator. He knows content and technology; he is obviously on good terms with the class. His equipment is state-of-the-art and he has a bright group of students. At least 80 or 90 percent have computers at home and use them regularly for schoolwork and game playing. Many of their parents work in technology industries. Yet the lesson leaves no one enthused, few able to cut and paste confidently, and most with only a sliver more knowledge of California regional geography than they entered with.

Perhaps it's a time problem. Computer class is just once a week for 45 minutes. Only a little can be learned in 45 minutes; lots can be forgotten in the intervening 167 hours and 15 minutes.

As the children finish the pasting activity, Bruce allows them to open a drawing program. I watch the screens as students quickly draw or scribble, changing colors and line weights and applying special effects. Are they creating art or killing time? It appears to be the latter. Are all of Bruce's classes like this? Every teacher has a bad day when a lesson doesn't work. And this lesson didn't seem to. I tell myself that it's too early to draw conclusions, and that I must continue to watch and listen.

The class ends, and students shut down the computers and exit, slinging their backpacks over their shoulders. Some packs are nearly a third the weight of the child carrying them. A few have wheels. Will the day come when all a child needs to carry is a tablet, a stylus, and a wireless modem?

▶ ▶ ▶

The next period is free for Bruce, so we'll have a chance to talk. He has arranged for me to visit classes at each level: kindergarten through 2nd grade, 3rd and 4th grade, and 5th and 6th grade. We sit down to talk but are interrupted by the arrival of a 5th grade teacher, Karen Evans. She looks weary, and for good reason.

"I was here in the lab until 10:00 p.m. last night, working on the grade book software. I won't let this thing beat me," she says with a tone of friendly determination. "The problem is I don't know how to use a computer, but I'm trying. By 10:00 last night I think I had it."

Bruce and Karen discuss her problem and the solution she came to. "You know more than you think," he tells her. "Keep fighting. You'll win."

It's clear that Bruce is infused with a can-do attitude. He sees himself as a service to teachers, students, and parents. For example, he built a user interface for the school's Web site, which contains links to relevant Internet sites. He updates it regularly, adding links to sites organized by curricular areas and topics and removing links that are no longer active. If a teacher wants to do a unit on endangered species, Bruce will research links and post them to the site, where they are available for teachers, students, and parents. He has also sent home information to parents on how to locate Web sites on topics their children are studying, like the California missions.

As Bruce and I talk, we are joined by another teacher, Randy Richardson. Randy is on vacation this term, and his classes are being covered by a recent graduate. Randy, Bruce tells me, is the faculty's most enthusiastic computer user. Bruce has asked him to come meet me. He also wanted Randy to give his class a pep talk on the importance of an upcoming computer activity on the water cycle. Bruce will conduct the activity, but he doubts the substitute's ability to motivate the students.

When Bruce and Randy used this activity last year, the class scored very well on a post-activity test. I asked them if they thought the computer-based lesson helped the students learn the substance of the lesson better than traditional methods.

"Definitely," says Randy. "The use and manipulation of graphic elements brought these kids closer to the content. I found a Web site with very good information and simulations about the water cycle. Bruce used it in his class, and the kids read more about the water cycle from a textbook. We use an old book from 1984. It works because the kids can read it. Our newer textbooks are a lot better-looking and crammed with a lot more information, but the reading levels are just too high for these kids."

I urge Randy to describe some other ways he uses technology.

"E-mail, for one," he replies. "It makes it easier for parents to contact me. But it's the same parents who contact me by note or phone call. E-mail's just more efficient for them. E-mail is easy because 85 percent of my kids have computers at home. A lot of them use computers for reports. They can get pretty elaborate, with a lot of different fonts, colors, and artwork. I don't give them extra credit for the way reports look, though."

My next question touches a sore spot: Does computer use help students perform better on tests?

"We test too much," Randy says with ill-concealed disdain. "Our state policy committees need to include more teachers and fewer politicians who don't have kids. I'm waiting for the pendulum to swing back away from testing. I hope I'll still be teaching when it does."

Bruce interrupts to tell me that Harrison's principal, Marshall Williams, has a short break in his schedule and wants to visit with me. We hurry over to the administrative building. I thank Marshall for allowing me to visit, and then pose my question about technology and test scores to him.

"I don't know if technology will help raise scores," Marshall answers. "That's really not why we've made the investment. We need technology because it's the tool of our age. Kids have to be good information users, and technology makes floods of information

available. Kids have to be taught how to filter it. We can't be com-
placent if we're going to teach them to live in the 21st century. Whatever technology's value, though, it will never replace good teaching."

The principal's phone rings, and our meeting is cut short.

► ► ►

Bruce and I walk out into the intense late-morning sun. Several 5th
grade classes are out for recess. The 90-degree heat does not dis-
courage a game of dodgeball. Small groups of girls huddle together
giggling. We walk into an empty 5th grade classroom to meet
teacher Michael Evans. Like Randy, he is on vacation this term, but
Bruce asked him to come in to meet me. Bruce had promised me a
parade of his technology superstars.

"Technology should be integral to everything we do in the classroom because we are in the 21st century," Michael says, echoing the
principal. "I use it every way I can." He goes on to say that he
started with two iMacs purchased from funds he qualifies for as a
mentor teacher. Each student in his classes spends two half-hour
sessions a week on one of these computers. They develop reports
using PowerPoint, produce their classroom newspaper, take photos
with a digital camera to serve as writing prompts, use algebra and
geometry drill-and-practice software to prepare for tests, and submit
a word-processed writing project every five to six weeks.

I ask Michael about the math practice software. Does the technology help the kids perform better?

"I don't know," he replies, "but I do know that we're pushing
kids too hard. We may be doing nothing but alienating them. And
tests are taking some of the fun out of teaching for me."

► ► ►

I'd like to hear more, but Bruce has scheduled lunch for me with a
group of teachers in the teachers' lounge. There are two tables in
the lounge. At one, a teacher sits reading Stephen King's *The Shining*. Beside her, another teacher studies the morning sports section.
A microwave oven buzzes, and a teacher removes a serving of re-
heated lasagna. Next to the microwave, a pot of coffee is brewing.

After quick introductions, I sit at a table with four teachers and invite them to tell me about how they use technology in their classes. This is what they have to say:

• Pat, 1st grade teacher: "I develop lesson plans and activity sheets on my home computer. I used to go home and use it every night. Now I don't have to because I've developed and saved these resources. It took a lot longer in the beginning, but now I'm saving time."

• Heather, 3rd grade teacher: "I use a reading motivation program that assigns kids points for each book they read. They take a test, and if they get 80 percent right, they get the points. The tests show me if the kids have read the books without the trouble of a book report. Book reports take so long for kids to complete. Plus, kids share information about books, so reports can be written without reading the books. These tests can't be fooled."

• Walter, 4th grade teacher: "Technology is a real problem, especially here at Harrison. We do a good job, but that's because of Bruce. Without him, we'd be dead in the water. The problem is that when we get kids from other schools, they don't have the skills that our kids do. Then we have to try to get them up to speed. Some kids come knowing how to use PCs. Then we have to get them up to speed on Macs. It can be a lot of trouble."

• Brenda, 4th grade teacher: "We followed the Tour de France. That was good for geography. I use my computer for e-mail too, but I've learned a lesson there. I won't open an e-mail around kids again. I opened one and it contained unsolicited pornography. I won't do that again."

▶ ▶ ▶

Bruce wants me to see the reading motivation program in action. I've seen it before but am interested in how Harrison Elementary uses it. We walk out into the afternoon sun, which has driven the heat to nearly 100 degrees. Relief comes as we enter Pam Borders's air-conditioned 5th grade classroom.

"Let me show you the test reports," Pam says, opening up a file drawer. In it are neatly organized folders arranged by student name and test period. She draws out a class report from a recently administered reading test that comes with the motivational program. To my surprise, the class's average reading level is below 5th grade. I had long thought that California's educational problems were linked to socioeconomic, linguistic, and cultural factors. But here, in an upper-income suburb, in classes with virtually no non-English speakers, the measured performance was well below expectations.

"People don't read today," Pam says. "There is too much competition for time. These kids come from families that don't read. The kids are into sports when they are outside and digital games and TV when they are inside. That's why I use this program. They get practice reading. We read an hour every day. Think what the average reading level would be if we didn't."

I don't like to think about it, and don't have to because the bell rings. Bruce and I go back to the computer lab, where he teaches the California regions lesson to another 4th grade class. It is a virtual replay of the morning session, with students having problems locating their files, finding the worksheet with their notes, and remembering how to cut and paste. Somewhere in all the mechanics, the content about regions is buried.

▶ ▶ ▶

When I leave Harrison that afternoon, I see Principal Marshall Williams standing at the curb of the school's sweeping driveway. He's directing children onto buses, saying hello to parents who have come for their children, and waving full buses on their way. Despite the heat, the children are animated, bubbling with noise and energy. As they step up into the buses, they lug their backpacks behind them. Why do I think all those books inside will go unread?

Viewpoint

I came away from Harrison with many positive impressions: The teachers were clearly committed to their students, the school was free of serious discipline problems, and parent support seemed good. Bruce Conrad, the technology coordinator, was hardworking, enthusiastic, and well liked. What's more, Bruce had good equipment to work with and a solid network infrastructure.

However, I was—and am—puzzled by the complexity of the technology Bruce chose to use. In the classes I observed, the students often seemed baffled as to what they should be doing. Had Bruce neglected to structure the class so it was fail-safe for the students? Was 45 minutes too little time in which to accomplish his goals? Was his lesson an appropriate match of instructional tools and instructional content? For example, Bruce was teaching draw, cut, paste, and save functions around the subject of California regional geography, but I don't think the students learned much about drawing, cutting, pasting, *or* geography. It also seemed to me that he was trying to teach the technology skills too quickly. But with such limited time and students who needed to learn so much, could more be expected?

A core problem with school technology use is the lack of a carefully developed curriculum plan that teaches skills at an appropriate age. I observed this at Harrison and at many other schools. "Integrate, integrate, integrate," teachers are urged. "Integrate computer use into the curriculum." Nevertheless, as I saw at Harrison and elsewhere, students must first learn fundamental skills.

There may be another problem here: play, or the perception of play. Conventional wisdom tells us that students take naturally to computers. Listening to children makes me believe that they take naturally to computer *games*. The Nintendo, PlayStation, and Xbox consoles are what students know best. These games have been expressly crafted to provide a fast-moving visual and auditory experience. The controls have been studied and perfected by human factors engineers. Kids connect with these games because companies have invested millions of dollars to ensure they fit the interests and abilities of kids (and adults). The games are highly intuitive.

Not so with Bruce's lesson on California regional geography. Not so with the computers' draw, cut, paste, and save functions. Bruce's iMacs are more intuitive than Windows machines, but they demand that users follow an unforgiving sequence of steps. Neither kids nor adults take to these steps naturally. The steps must be taught with structure, care, and abundant opportunity for practice. This will not happen in 45-minute, once-a-week computer lab sessions that *also* must incorporate social studies, language arts, and other content area instruction.

And in this sense, my visit to Harrison was one more indication that time, or lack of it, is a core reason that computers have negligible impact on measured student performance. Consideration of the time problem leads to the question of what applications schools might find so compelling that teachers and administrators would *want* children to use a computer for more than an hour a week.

▶▶▶ 12

Woodvale
Middle School

"I LOVE THESE KIDS. THAT BOX DOESN'T LOVE THESE KIDS."

A tear glistens in Rosemary Lawton's eye. Rosemary, in her early 50s, has been teaching for nearly three decades. She points at a computer in the corner of her 7th grade classroom. Her hand shakes visibly. "I am a very good teacher. I am not a 'facilitator.' But I'm beginning to feel that I'm not a good teacher. Am I making sense?" she asks plaintively.

I'm at Woodvale Middle School, in an upper-class suburb of a major southeastern city. The school's technology coordinator has scheduled me to meet with computer users and nonusers, fans and critics. Rosemary tells me that she wants to be a user and a believer.

"I've tried. God knows I've tried. I've taken workshops on PowerPoint and on how to make Web pages, but they spend all of their time on background, borders, and glitz, not on substance. They talk about animation and sound effects, not content. School should be about substance, not style; about content, not glitz. Am I making sense?" she asks again.

"I hear all this talk about centers in the classroom. I don't need centers in my classroom; I'm the center. These are *my* kids, not the computer's. I'm their teacher, not a facilitator. I'm teaching them to think and to read, not to push buttons. Does that make sense?" she asks once more.

"Kids can't do anything on their own anymore," Rosemary says. "They become frustrated if they can't find answers immediately. All they want to do is point and click, cut and paste. We're not teaching them to process on their own."

I think of Rosemary's words as I head to my next destination, a 6th grade social studies class taught by Erin Campbell. Erin is directing a unit on European countries. A recorded summary of the lesson plays from an audio CD. The narrator describes the geographical features of Europe as Erin points to them on a wall map. "These are visual and aural learners," Erin explains. *Can they read?* I wonder

I notice a Hispanic girl listening to an audio description in Spanish. "She speaks very little English," Erin tells me, "so she listens to the tape several times."

The narration finishes, and the students move to clusters of desks. One group works on a multiple-choice quiz. Erin tells them to narrow the choices to two and then select the one that seems best. "That's the way you should do it on the proficiencies," she reminds the students.

A second group works on essays about the European country they chose to study. "Don't take these home," she tells the group. "I don't want your parents helping. I'm confident you can do these. And remember to use similes and metaphors in your writing." This is a cross-curricular unit, Erin explains to me, integrating social studies and writing.

As the quiz takers finish, they move to six computers lined against the wall in the back of the classroom. Erin's desk is in the back as well. On it is a laptop computer she uses to control a large-screen monitor at the front of the classroom. The monitor is off today, but Erin often uses it to find Web sites related to the subject being studied.

Four of the six computers are in use. At one, a boy searches the Web for information about Monaco, the country he is studying. At the others, three boys use a graphics program to make "adoption" certificates. As part of the unit, they have adopted a European country, and the certificates confirm that adoption. The boys compare the colors, type styles, borders, and special graphic effects they have chosen for their certificates.

Back in the 7th grade class, Rosemary told me, "These kids come from Erin's class with all her technology and I just feel awful. It frustrates me because I don't have the time for it. Teaching is getting to know the students and watching the light bulbs go on. That's teaching."

Which of these teachers is right? I wonder. Or are they both partly right? The classes are like Rorschach inkblots. You see in them what you are predisposed to see. Without measurement data, I can't tell which teacher accomplishes the most. Maybe their true accomplishments can't be measured.

► ► ►

Laura Winston, Woodvale's technology coordinator, has mapped out a full day for me. Several of my classroom visits are scheduled for teacher planning periods. That means I'll see the teachers, but not their students. That's a disappointment, but I can't do anything about it now.

Laura has been at Woodvale for three years. "When I came," she says, "we had three labs plus one computer for every 250 kids. Now, the labs are mostly used to teach keyboarding to 6th graders. The vocational ed teachers who teach it have salaries funded through a special state program. When the labs aren't used for typing, teachers can sign up their classes. They are not often free, so most of kids' computer time is on their classroom machines."

Laura is a strong advocate of partnering with business. Before coming to Woodvale, she worked with a statewide public policy group, setting up partnerships between business and schools. She brought those skills to Woodvale. "Before I went to the public policy group, I was a change agent at a middle school," Laura says. "A large local pharmaceutical company was worried about the poor quality of the school. They felt it hurt their ability to recruit. My job was to create a school for at-risk kids within the school. We used technology to focus on their special needs. I had a three-year grant to make it work. The idea was to migrate technology from the high-risk, special needs classes to the entire school. In a year and a half, the job was done. That's when I moved on."

► ► ►

My next stop is a 7th grade language arts class, where teacher Stuart Lawson is teaching a poetry unit. Today the students are reading revised drafts of sonnets to small three- or four-person writing circles. Preteen girls read breathless lines that quiver with barely suppressed sexual innuendo. Boys smirk and exchange knowing glances. An in-class reading resource teacher guides two special-needs students who work on a separate assignment.

"Each student has an online mentor, who is a community volunteer," Stuart explains. "The student sends the mentor a poem, and the mentor critiques and returns it. We have an e-mail address for the class. The students use numbers, not names, so the mentors don't know who their students are. Each mentor works with two or three students. We train the mentors online and provide them with rubrics and sample poems. By working with several students, they can compare the work and come to know what to expect of students. Mentoring is a good way for us to involve the community."

"Does it help the students learn to write better?" I ask.

"Yes, especially lower-performing students," Stuart answers. "I do this unit early in the year, and the special attention keeps them motivated. They like the technology, and they like the personal attention."

Stuart is a veteran teacher in his 21st year on the job. He taught for two years in Wisconsin and was then recruited to this rapidly growing area of the Southeast. "People here are attuned to technology," he says. "I really started using technology when I discovered an electronic grade book. It was so much better than paper. It really helped me analyze how kids were doing, to uncover their strengths and weaknesses."

Pursuing my overarching theme of technology's influence on measured performance, I ask Stuart if technology has helped his students do better on state proficiency tests. He thinks so. Technology, he tells me, appeals to a wide variety of learning styles: "Some kids prefer to read from a computer. They like the immediate feedback it offers. Drill-and-practice programs can motivate students who otherwise wouldn't learn the basics. The Web opens up whole new areas for research."

Stuart uses a reading motivation program with five students who perform below grade level. He is convinced that the motivated reading practice helps their reading skills. He admires many other software programs, but he can't just bring them into his classroom. The tech support department must approve any software used on a school computer. They check it out and mount it, after ensuring that the program doesn't conflict with any existing software. But Stuart is always looking for new and better things. "Technology is something you can't ignore," he tells me as I leave his classroom. "It is coming; you either embrace it or fall behind."

Stuart walks me to the door, and I head to Rita Donaldson's social studies class, dodging students as they chatter at lockers lining the halls. Barely 5 feet tall, Rita is in her mid-50s and has taught for 25 years. Her career took her to China on a Fulbright Fellowship and included four years with the state Department of Education. She is experienced and energetic.

"People don't have to tell me I'm short. I've already figured that out," she says, drawing an analogy to using technology with slower students. "That's what they think when we make them use those awful remedial software programs. Forcing kids to use this type of material sends the wrong message and accomplishes nothing. It is repetitive and boring.

"Technology is just not simple. There are so many components that can break. If the technology is cumbersome for teachers, they won't use it," Rita observes. "I'm afraid we are trying to sell a bill of goods to the American public if we think technology is the answer to our problems."

Rita is no Luddite. She says the Internet is the "most powerful tool ever invented, even though it has problems." In a unit last year, Rita used a site on the Salem witch trials, and she plans to use it again this year.

Rita thinks part of the problem is the state of technology itself and part is training. "I took 25 hours of computer training, but I learned more from two of my 8th grade students. Some of the software is just too complicated, even for the kids. They need an adult aide or volunteer to be involved. The teacher can't pay attention to kids on the computers and to the class at the same time.

"Most of the software I see is flash with no substance. But the Internet, that's another matter. As a research tool, it's great for me. I find lots of material for lessons that would not be available to me in books. I love it."

Viewpoint

Conventional wisdom says that veteran teachers avoid technology while new teachers embrace it. This was not what I found at Woodvale and other schools. Teachers in general were not computer phobic, whatever their experience, although I did meet some veteran teachers who didn't want the trouble of learning something new—especially something that seemed to demand so much energy.

Many teachers, both veteran and new, used computers for planning, research, and administrative tasks. I observed and spoke with teachers who developed lesson plans on their computers, going to the Web for resources and information. They saved time by archiving and retrieving these lesson plans. They also used computers for grade books and record keeping.

Use of the computer as an administrative and productivity tool did not necessarily lead to its effective use as an instructional tool. New teachers who grew up with computers were often focusing on the complexities of teaching and the challenges of classroom management. Integrating computers ranked rather far down on their priority lists. Some new teachers enthusiastically used computers in the classroom, but to little effect. They knew how to use computers but had not yet learned enough about instruction to use them well. Their lessons could be long on glitz, but short on substance.

On the other hand, veteran teachers who understood instruction and embraced technology taught some of the most effective classes that I observed. They knew their content, knew their students, and knew how to support lessons through technology. They did not feel compelled to use technology for its own sake. It was a servant of the content, not a substitute for it.

▶▶▶ 13

City Academy

"OUR SCORES PLUMMETED BECAUSE OUR DEMOGRAPHICS CHANGED," says Assistant Principal Jim Douglas. Jim is sitting in his office at City Academy, a K–12 public school in New England. He has been part of City Academy from its beginning 10 years ago. The school follows a reform model financed by the New American Schools program, a privately funded, nonprofit organization that since 1991 has organized corporations to invest $100 million toward the conceptualization and testing of new models for schooling.

"City Academy's model emphasizes project-based learning, a participative administrative structure, use of technology, and a small, K–12 school environment," Jim explains to me. "Our challenge in the last couple of years has been to maintain the integrity of our model in an era of standards and high-stakes testing."

Jim goes on to tell me how the idea of City Academy emerged. A former teacher of the gifted and talented, he and another administrator in his district dreamed of creating a school for all students that was based on the principles used in the education of the gifted and talented. The school would launch a constructivist-inspired curriculum built around projects.

Like the convergence of weather patterns that cause a perfect storm, City Academy as it exists today is the result of several educational patterns coming together in unexpected ways. At the beginning, everything seemed to go right. As Jim and his administrator friend mulled over the prospects of a new school, a corporation that had developed a winning reform model through the New American Schools program was looking for a pilot project. The concepts were a great fit. With a source of funds and support from their district, Jim and some colleagues set out to transform an existing inner-city K–5 school into their vision of what education could and should be. That was City Academy.

The school soon expanded, adding 6th, 7th, and 8th grades at a separate location. Later, grades 9 through 12 were added at a third location, bringing the total City Academy enrollment to 850 students. The school was putting together a solid academic record. Test scores were at the upper range for urban schools and each year they saw measurable progress.

"What we did in the early '90s was cutting-edge," Jim tells me. "Some of it, like multimedia project-based learning, is mainstream today. But there have been tensions and stresses between our vision and the standards and high-stakes testing movement," he tells me. "We have had to modify our project-based approach to align with new content guidelines and testing."

In the mid-1990s, City Academy leaders made plans to consolidate all three locations into a single campus. Using federal, state, and district funds, they built a new, state-of-the-art building on the inner-city site of the original K–5 school. The transition was more difficult than school leaders could have imagined and highlighted the conflict between the school's project-based model and the realities of the accountability era.

"That first year was spent just trying to survive," Jim says. "We were designed for 850, but 1,000 students showed up. This is an open enrollment district, and parents wanted their kids here. This building was a real magnet, but it attracted many new, lower-performing students. And our test scores showed it."

"Let me show you around," he says, moving from behind his desk. "I'll show you what we are doing to bring test scores up."

Jim explains that City Academy has invested heavily in a technology-supported reading program, which was developed at a respected university and has gone through extensive field trials. Although not project-based, the program is rooted in the latest cognitive research and uses a range of traditional and new media. It is the instructional centerpiece of City Academy's school improvement plan. A lot is riding on it.

Then Jim breaks the bad news. "I'm afraid that there is a lot I *can't* show you on your visit today," he says. "Our network has been down for two weeks."

As we walk through the finely appointed building, Jim describes the network problem. A serious virus that made headline news as it attacked corporate, government, and home computers also invaded the school's network. Technical support personnel are working to restore it, but the problem is complicated because the school's network is part of the municipal network. City government offices are down as well, and Jim knows that entities like law enforcement and the bureau of motor vehicles have priority over the schools.

How, I wonder, *does a curriculum that is built around technology function when the network is frozen for two weeks?* I soon learn the answer: Not very well.

▶ ▶ ▶

My first visit is with Janet Crosswell, director of the K–5 video department. City Academy's core technology was originally television. That technology focus has shifted to computers, but the school still broadcasts student-created programs. The district also sponsors a public access channel that broadcasts educational programs to parents and the community.

"We model parenting skills and demonstrate ways that parents can help their children learn to read," Janet tells me. "Many of our parents didn't get much support at home when they were children. We try to use TV to model for them. Parents will tell us, 'We didn't know we could do that.' We help open the door for them. And they like seeing their kids on TV.

"Ours is a highly visual population. They have to see things and do things. Many of our students come to school with very little experience in life. We offer as many tactile, aural, kinesthetic, and visual experiences as possible," she explains.

But there are no visual experiences on City Academy's computer screens today. That's a problem for art teacher Jennifer Lippman: "I depend on museum sites for prints and on art material sites for activities. Being locked out of both really hurts. I just hope we are back up soon."

This is a sentiment shared by Jonell Dawson, the 10th grade integrated science teacher whose class I visit with Janet. "I use a lot of PowerPoint presentations for life science and biology demonstrations," Jonell says. "I feel lost without them. And I have curriculum units saved from last year that I can't access. I'm making do, but it's not the same."

I ask Jonell about faculty inservice programs. Has she taken any courses online? And if so, what has the virus done to them? Jonell replies that she has taken two courses from the Smithsonian, one on cloning and one on the diversity of fish—and both prior to the virus episode. Then I ask if she found the contact with other students in the online courses worthwhile. "There was no contact," she says. "All of my study partners quit. I understand there is a high dropout rate. The courses were a lot of work, but they were quite worthwhile."

▸ ▸ ▸

My next stop is the middle school reading lab to see what I can of the technology-supported reading program. The program mixes whole-group instruction, individual tutoring, CD-ROMs, and audiotapes. The CD-ROMs contain interactive exercises, video clips, and assessments.

"We can make this a very personal program," says Meg Fisher, the lab director. "It offers a good mix of technology, independent reading, whole-group instruction, and one-on-one tutoring.

"Of course, we can't use the computers now," she continues, "and that hurts. I'm at home with hardware, so I can usually take care of things when the network is up. I've taught computer literacy to adults and I'm not afraid to dig into hardware problems. That helps a lot in this job. I get called on to do a lot of fixes with this program."

There are 12 students in the room. Four of them sit on two large, gray, imitation leather sofas. All four students wear headphones, which are connected to audio players that rest on their laps. On one sofa, two boys are kicking at one another; they are holding books, but not looking at them. A girl sits with eyes barely open, the closed book resting on her stomach. Another boy focuses on his book intently, following the text and listening.

Meg calls to the kickers, telling them to pay attention. "Thank you for cooperating," she says, as they quit their kicking. Looking back at me, Meg says, "We are usually better organized, but with the system down we have to change what we do. The kids are motivated by the computers. It is hard to get that same motivation every day in a classroom."

I glance back at the boys. They are kicking again. Meg ignores them and starts to show me one of the program's reports. "These reports tell me a lot about each student, but I wish the program had a phonics component. These kids need phonics. I understand it is going to be added."

The bell rings, and the students start to put away their books and recorders. Meg walks to the doorway. As each student leaves, she gives them a sticker and says, "Thank you for cooperating today." As the kickers approach, she says to the remaining students, "Some of you did not cooperate. You know who you are." Then she gives stickers to the kickers anyway as they pass through the door.

"I wish I could have shown you more," Meg says as I start to leave. "Maybe you can come back when the network is up."

► ► ►

Back in Assistant Principal Jim Douglas's office, he talks of his hopes for the reading program: "We've learned we can't do everything around projects. Now we do projects in the afternoon. We hope the new program will help our kids develop the skills they need. Struggling readers are a real concern."

Jim elaborates on how City Academy has had to shift its reading program away from a whole-language, heavily constructivist approach. "At one time, we tried to use just trade books," he says. "Trade books were the core of all our reading instruction. We tried to integrate trade books into our projects and build our reading program on the projects and the books. That was too ambitious."

"We also start modestly and increase project work as students move through the grades. There are fewer projects in the primary grades, but more in the middle grades.

"We've modified our math program as well," Jim continues. "We originally organized math classes not by grade level but by student performance, mixing students from a three-grade span. This year we went back to a graded program. We think we'll be better able to align instruction with proficiency test requirements."

I leave City Academy at day's end. Several days later, I receive an e-mail from Jim. After three weeks, the network is finally back up.

Viewpoint

"Testing is our driving force," said a teacher at Lambert Elementary School, which I describe in Chapter 15. Every teacher at City Academy could say the same thing. So could most teachers at the other schools I visited. To a great degree, state standards, and the tests designed to measure their mastery, drive the actions of today's administrators and teachers.

This reality was most obvious at City Academy. The school's original pedagogical principles occupied the opposite end of the spectrum from the test-driven standards movement. Until recent years, City Academy's project-based approach produced students who scored at or above students with similar socioeconomic profiles. Then, according to Assistant Principal Jim Douglas, a population shift occurred and things began to change.

Throughout its history, City Academy had worked to adjust and fine-tune its approach. The project-based approach was modified, multigrade grouping for math was abandoned, and heavy investment was made in a more structured reading program. This research-based program promised measurable growth, which City Academy urgently needed. The program was designed around contemporary theories of cognitive science, but it still operated far from City Academy's project-based foundations.

In other schools I visited, the tension between theoretical principles and instructional reality was even more dramatic. Technology-using teachers found themselves at the center of that tension. On one hand, they were urged by technology leaders to use computers as tools for constructivist pedagogy. On the other, they experienced intense pressure to prepare students for tests, often using test preparation methods based on behaviorist principles.

Constructivism is the dominant theory that underlies the technology movement. One technology consultant I met quoted a superintendent who jokingly told her, "You should be bound by truth-in-advertising laws." He recognized the intimate relationship between constructivism and the technology movement. The tension that teachers felt sprang from conflicting calls to use constructivist-inspired computer activities within a behaviorist-driven, high-stakes environment.

Instruction rooted in a constructivist pedagogy takes time. According to constructivist theory, learners create their own knowledge. They explore, invent, question, and create. They are not passive recipients of information and formulas. Technology leaders, who often shape the strategic visions for district technology plans, regularly disparage test prep and drill-and-practice programs. Yet teachers find themselves called to use these programs, especially in schools that fall at or below acceptable performance levels. Theory and reality clash, and teachers are the ones who feel the bruises. When I heard teachers say, "I don't have time for technology" or "If it is a choice between preparing for the math proficiency or going to computer lab, I'll do math prep," they were articulating that dilemma.

At the beginning of my study, I had a hunch that a core reason for technology's failure to influence measured performance was that technology products and methods were not grounded in a consistent, articulated learning theory. My school observations showed me it was not that simple. I learned that there are, in fact, two conflicting learning theories: constructivism, which shapes the technology vision, and behaviorism, which shapes the political reality. When push came to shove, most administrators and teachers I observed accepted the political reality.

► ► ►   # 14

Emerson
Elementary School

I'M HEADING NORTH OUT OF BOSTON. EARLY MORNING TRAFFIC clogs the southbound lanes of the interstate highway. Near the New Hampshire border, I turn off and follow a series of pine-bordered rural roads. Real estate signs point to new residential developments: Lake Forest Estates, Sherwood Forest, Singing Brook Manors. The names signal the changing character of these rural acres as they become home to Massachusetts and New Hampshire commuters.

The school population is surging in Brookside, the once-quiet New England town that I am visiting. I pull into the parking lot of Emerson Elementary School, nestled against a backdrop of pines. At the left of the single-story red brick building is a play area with a variety of young children's play equipment.

This year, Emerson houses kindergarten, 1st grade, 2nd grade, and 3rd grade. Next year, the classes will move to a new building now under construction. Fourth and 5th grade students now housed in a building three miles away will join them. Emerson will then become a regional center for special education classes. In the meantime, the district is playing musical buildings as it copes with the changing demographics of the community.

▸ ▸ ▸

In the Emerson office, the school secretary hands me a visitor sticker and then leads me through a combination gym, lunchroom, and music classroom. At several tables, handfuls of young children who qualify for a federal breakfast program finish their cereal, juice, and fruit.

Karen Edwards, the school's technology coordinator, sits at her desk in an area shared by the school media director. She glances through some accumulated mail and announcements. Karen and I have e-mailed and spoken by phone, so introductions are brief.

"I was away yesterday," she tells me, "so I have some catching up to do." She goes on to say that she was at a special education team meeting. In addition to her duties as Emerson's technology coordinator, Karen lends technology support to district special education programs. At yesterday's workshop, she and some of her colleagues took their first look at some newly acquired assistive devices for special-needs students. The Brookside district has one student who uses a Braille reader. Others use special devices for hearing, mobility, and partial-sight disabilities. The day's workshop brought together representatives from special ed, technical support, and speech therapy, along with several classroom teachers, administrators, and paraprofessionals. They discussed tools and strategies for further integrating special-needs students into regular classrooms.

"Technology is opening doors for these students," Karen says, referring to children with a variety of disabilities. "It is important that everyone involved understand what technology can do. That's why we got the grant for this equipment and for yesterday's workshop. Technology can make a difference for these kids, and everyone who works with them has to understand that."

As Karen and I talk, a group of 1st graders comes in with their teacher. This is their weekly library day. Above the hum of children's voices, I hear Brenda Weckesser, the media center director. "Hurry up," she says. "Choose your books, and then you can play some computer games." The 15 children move from shelf to shelf, picking out books and paging through them.

"Here's Lyle," a boy says with delight.

"I want this Arthur book," says another.

"Hurry, now," the media director says. "We're going to vote on the software."

The students gather around her. Several peek at the pages of their books. Brenda holds a handful of CD-ROMs for the students to see. They will vote on which ones to mount to the media center computers. The winners are Green Eggs and Ham, Arthur's Computer Adventure, Kid Pix, and Arthur's Birthday.

Pairs of children settle in front of the center's four computers. Two boys walk to a table, open their books, and begin to read silently. Two other boys and three girls choose photocopies from a stack of coloring worksheets, gather crayons, and begin to color.

I move over to watch a boy and girl sitting before a computer. On the screen is a word: "shoe." Below it are three pictures: a mailbox, a ladder, and a shoe. The little girl clicks on the shoe.

"I'm going to win," she laughs as a score shows on the screen.

"You beat me," acknowledges the little boy mildly, with no sense of defeat.

"Oh good, you guys are having fun," says Brenda, who stands next to me, watching.

The two children finish with the computer and exchange places with the students at the coloring table. Students at the two other computers rotate also. The two boys who have been reading relinquish their books and sit down at keyboards.

When the period ends, the students gather their materials, and the teacher shepherds them out. A new group enters. Brenda greets them with a question: "Are you ready to have some fun?"

Later, she and I talk about the classes. "We play the games to allow the children to get familiar with the computers," the media center director says. "As they get comfortable, we'll start to integrate computer use into the curriculum. We *work* on the computer; we don't play on it."

Karen doesn't see my puzzled look, but she picks up Brenda's point: "We use technology to do things we could not do without it, or that a computer does better. And every activity relates to our state framework."

▸ ▸ ▸

I should get an example of that at Karen's next class. We walk to a 1st grade room, where Karen introduces me to the teacher, Kim Davis. Karen goes to the front of the room and sits on a small chair beside a low-slung table. On the table is an iMac. The 21 students settle on the carpet before her, and I sit down with them.

Karen is demonstrating a program that allows the user to drag and drop a variety of single-colored geometric shapes. The shapes are arranged at the bottom of the screen. Karen explains how the mouse controls the cursor, enabling her to move the shapes one by one around the screen. Her lesson is about symmetry.

"How many eyes do you have? How many legs? How many arms?" With each answer, she drags and places the geometric parts until the screen shows a symmetrical stick figure body.

With the demonstration completed, eight children go in pairs to the classroom's four computers. Kim directs the remaining students to other activities while Karen coaches the computer users.

At one computer, a boy effortlessly drags rectangles, circles, and triangles to make a non-representational geometric figure. It looks like a computer-generated Rorschach blot. Next to him, a small girl struggles with the coordination needed to drag and drop. Karen places her hand over the girl's fingers, and together they guide the mouse. The girl looks troubled as Kim directs her to create a mirror-image on the screen.

"Do you know what to do?" Karen asks the girl.

The girl doesn't respond. I see that at the next computer, another girl has assembled a figure that looks like a dog. It is not symmetrical, but it is recognizable.

This is October, and Halloween is nearing. Karen suggests to the students that they use the geometric shapes to make scary monsters when they have their next turn on the computers. The children rotate from the computers to their desks and back. By class's end, all 21 have had a turn. Leaving the room, I notice a set of geometric wooden blocks, which have been sitting unused throughout the period.

► ► ►

Karen and I enter another 1st grade room. These are the same children I saw in the library. Milk crates full of paperback picture and reading books line two walls of the classroom. A rolling cart is positioned at the front of the room, and plugged into slots on the cart are 20 electronic keyboards with small, built-in LED screens. Karen and the teacher, Fran Bascom, give a keyboard to each student. The students sit on the floor in front of Karen. I see that the four-line LED screens display letters as the keys are depressed. The children have used the keyboards before, and they know how to depress the keys.

In this class, Karen is using technology to teach about capital letters. She explains the purpose of the shift key and asks, "When do we use a capital letter?"

"On my name," says one child.

"At the beginning of a sentence," says another.

Karen depresses the shift key, enters a letter, and shows it to the class. The children strain to see the small display. "Do it yourself," she encourages. "Depress the shift key and type the letter M."

The children try it, and I look over their shoulders at the Ms on the displays. "This is cool," a boy speaks up.

"It's like my laptop at home," says another.

The children move back to their desks, each carrying a keyboard and a sheet of paper with words printed on it. Karen instructs them to type the words on their sheet. They do, slowly searching out each letter. Then they take the keyboards to Karen, who attaches them to a cord on the iMac, explaining that she is saving what they wrote to the hard drive of the computer. The children wait impatiently. By the time the class ends, all the typing has been saved, and the keyboards have been returned to the cart.

"I stick with principles," Karen tells me on the way back to her office. "I teach concepts about computers, not just mechanics. Computers in the future will be very different from what we have today. We can't get caught up with the mechanics."

▶ ▶ ▶

As we walk through the halls of Emerson, I sneak looks into 15 separate classrooms; all have classroom computers, but none of these computers are on. Children and teachers look busy with reading, math, science, and other subjects. Walls outside several classrooms show some computer output: digital photos of smiling children with decorative borders.

"I held an inservice session on how to use the digital camera," Karen tells me. Twice weekly she offers hour-long technology talks for the staff, covering topics like using a spreadsheet for grading, creating Web sites, teaching word processing, inserting graphics, and using Kid Pix and other software programs. She also provides one-on-one instruction and supports teachers in their classrooms, as I have seen today.

What, I wonder, has all this effort accomplished? Is it an efficient use of resources? Karen has done many things right according to the standards of technology leaders. Is it heresy to suggest this resource use is not efficient?

Viewpoint

Equity is a sacred value in U.S. public education. States struggle with funding formulas that support the equitable distribution of tax revenues. Districts set policies to ensure that schools in one part of the district do not have greater resources than schools in another. The results are imperfect, but the principle of equity guides educational policy.

From what I saw at Emerson and other schools, that policy should be reconsidered as far as computers are concerned. It's likely that every child at Emerson uses a computer at some time during the course of regular weekly activities. For example, I saw 1st graders play educational games in the media center, learn the rudiments of typing on a detachable keyboard, and create figures with drag-and-drop geometric shapes. The classroom teacher, the technology coordinator, and the media center director all supported this instruction.

Suppose the instruction had not been equitable. Suppose that Karen's special ed team had recommended that all the school's computers—not just the new assistive devices—be used primarily by special-needs and struggling students. Would focusing technology resources on the few with greatest needs have led to significant overall gains, without substantive loss to the many? Couldn't the lesson on geometric shapes have been taught just as well using the wooden blocks? Couldn't pencil and paper have been used as efficiently as electronic keyboards to teach rules of capitalization?

At Harriet Tubman Elementary School (see Chapter 2), I saw technology resources focused on a handful of children during a summer session. The groups were small, as few as six or eight children. The teachers knew the computer program, worked with the performance data it provided, and supported the computer's instruction with one-on-one teaching. The teachers received strong leadership from their principal and used a program with superior production values that engaged visual, aural, and kinesthetic ways of learning.

Skeptics may counter that Harriet Tubman represents an ideal situation, not replicable in most schools or districts. Yet, Harriet Tubman was a very low-income school, served transient families with 33 percent yearly turnover, and held class in sweltering mid-July weather. How ideal is that? The difference between Harriet Tubman and many other schools I visited was intense focus, vision, and leadership.

Karen was obviously experienced with computer operations. What might she achieve at Emerson if she focused her efforts on students at the low end of the performance curve? Intense service to struggling and special-needs students would come at the expense of the majority, but I left Emerson convinced that the benefit enjoyed by the majority was negligible at best. Every child got a little bit, but too little to have measurable impact. At Emerson, and other schools I visited, demand for equity diluted the impact that computer technology could deliver.

▶ ▶ ▶ # 15

Lambert Elementary School

LAMBERT ELEMENTARY SCHOOL LIES ON THE OUTSKIRTS OF A major southern city. It houses more than 1,100 students. Modular classrooms supplement Lambert's two-story building. A new classroom wing was added this year, but the modular buildings remain— kept to handle escalating enrollments.

Testing is a big focus here. A state-mandated high-stakes testing program rewards high-performing schools and sanctions schools that fail to meet performance goals. Lambert is a high-performing school, and last year, each teacher took home a $750 pay bonus.

"The tests are our driving force," 2nd grade teacher Maryanne Clements confirms as we sit in the teachers' lounge before the school day begins. Also at the table are two 3rd grade teachers and the school's technology coordinator, Julie Lawton.

I ask whether keyboarding is taught at Lambert. "No, it gives way to math," Maryanne tells me. The other teachers nod. "If you have the choice of providing keyboarding instruction or math preparation, it is going to be math. Our kids will learn keyboarding in middle school."

Spring proficiency tests are a constant reference point during my Lambert visit. I ask the group how technology affects test performance. "We don't know," Julie replies. "Our technology investment isn't based on test performance. We just know kids today need technology."

"Parents want it, too," adds Carol Masters, a 3rd grade teacher. "I had my class do reports using PowerPoint. They had to choose a country and then find information about its food, religion, family life, and entertainment. We showed the PowerPoint presentations at a parents' open house. The parents were impressed that their kids could do them."

"Computers help kids feel important," interjects Maryanne, "and they might help year-end test performance by nurturing critical thinking."

"We use computers with our motivational reading program," says Belinda Short, the other 3rd grade teacher. "Twenty-five percent of our reading grade is based on how many books they read and how well they score on the computerized tests. The kids just love the computer reports. I find the information on comprehension and accuracy very valuable. Here at Lambert, kids need 80 percent right to get credit on a book test. The reports tell me exactly what the kids have done."

▸ ▸ ▸

We wrap up our conversation, and I accompany Belinda to her classroom, where some students will start the day by taking a computerized reading comprehension test. While Belinda takes roll and handles morning administrative details, I move to the back of the room. I count 20 students: 3 are Asian, 5 are black, and the balance are white. There are 11 girls and 9 boys.

"If you've finished a book, take the test now," Belinda tells the class. Four students move quickly to the four computers that sit on tables in the back, where I am standing. Three other students, not as quick, return to their seats and wait.

At a computer to my left, a girl slides into a chair. She types in her last name: *Nguyen*. A school roster appears. It shows seven

Nguyens. She highlights her name: *Nguyen, Lien.* Then she types in the name of her book, laboriously searching out each letter: *H-o-r-r-i-b-l-e-H-a-r-r-y-a-n-d-t-h-e-D-r-o-p-o-f-D-o-o-m.* With a click of the mouse, a five-question quiz appears.

Quickly, Lien answers five multiple-choice questions, clicking with assurance on each. Five for 5, 100 percent, the screen shows. She then gets up, walks to the printer and waits while a report emerges. She smiles, returns to the computer, opens a folder of papers, inserts the report, and returns to her desk with a noticeable spring in her step.

Another girl takes her place. She finds her name, then types *T-h-e-N-a-p-p-i-n-g-H-o-u-s-e.* Another quiz, another five for five, another report, another springy step back to her desk.

"It's not the be-all-and-end-all," Belinda tells me, when I ask about the value of this program. "It is just another way to reach out to these kids and get them interested. It is an addition to our reading program, and the reports are very helpful."

▶ ▶ ▶

Belinda has started her reading class. I quietly exit and find my way to the computer lab on the first floor. For the past two years Julie, the tech coordinator, has taught a lesson on spreadsheets. Today, she will watch as the classroom teacher, Beth Anderson, teaches that lesson.

Julie stands in the back with me, ready to help. Computers on tables ring three sides of the room. Beth sits at the front, a computer on a table to her left. Thirteen 5th graders sit on the floor at her feet. Another 13 are back in their regular classroom with a student teacher. Both groups are studying topics from earth science.

Today's lesson focuses on entering data and generating graphs to show visual comparisons. Students will first set up spreadsheets and then enter data. Each student has a photocopy with information on earthquakes and their Richter scale ratings.

Beth opens a new spreadsheet and discusses the distinction between horizontal and vertical. She also refreshes the class on the distinction between the Richter scale (a measure of the energy given off by a quake) and the Mercali scale (a measure of damage). In

Column A of her spreadsheet, she enters the date and location of four earthquakes. She begins to type a column heading for the Richter measurement, but the cell is too narrow for "Richter," and she is stymied on how to expand it.

"Mrs. Anderson is still learning about computers," she explains to the class.

A student quickly explains how to expand the cell, and Beth completes her form. She then pairs the students and assigns them to the computers, where they will set up spreadsheets of their own. Two boys work together near me. They are uncertain how to highlight a cell in order to enter data. They speak quietly to each other, find the solution, enter the titles in the horizontal and vertical cells, and enter the data. They type slowly and carefully.

As they finish, Beth calls the class to the front of the room. She has entered data into her spreadsheet and is ready to produce horizontal and vertical bar graphs. They spend the balance of the class period creating these graphs. Colors and font choices are discussed at length. Decisions are made about bar width and title placement. Only briefly do they discuss which was the most powerful earthquake, which the least. They don't speculate on the reasons.

Afterward, I ask Beth why so much attention was given to the form of the data and so little to the substance. What benefit does knowing how to make a spreadsheet have if it does not support analysis and understanding of the content? I confess that to me, this lesson seemed to be about the mechanics of a spreadsheet, not about earth science and earthquakes.

"The activity is sort of contrived," Beth acknowledges, "but they will have to know how to make spreadsheets in 6th grade. I'm not sure if that is a state or a district requirement, but they'll have to know it. We're giving them a head start."

I understand the explanation, but I wonder about the priorities.

▸ ▸ ▸

The 5th graders leave, and a 4th grade class enters the lab. They will work on a math remediation program that the district makes available. Each student is assigned a lesson based on previous accomplishment. When they complete their lesson, they can use a drawing program.

I stand behind a young boy who is doing a lesson on how to read graphs. A graph appears on the screen, followed by a multiple-choice question. The boy guesses *A*, then *B*, and then *C*. His third guess, *C,* is correct. Next to him, a second boy works on his own lesson, but he seems distracted by the first boy's graph lesson on the screen next to him. His eyes dart from one screen to the other. Although his attention is divided, he still answers every question correctly.

Meanwhile, the boy with the graph lesson continues to guess at each question until he gets the right answer. He seems equally indifferent to the message that he is wrong and the encouraging words that appear when he clicks a right answer.

A third boy works on addition problems. He fingers the keys inattentively. He appears unmotivated to finish his lesson or to get the answers right. He glances occasionally at the monitors of students who have gone on to play with the graphics program.

I drift over to see how the students are using this graphics program. One student makes squiggly lines and then fills any closed loops with color. Another student makes random patterns of stars, much like rubber stamping on a sheet of paper. Some may see this as free play, unfettered creativity, or artistic discovery. To me, it looks like killing time. Knowing the school's focus on test performance, I wonder how this class contributes to Lambert's strategic goals. I also wonder whether students are concerned about their spring test performance.

"It's the parents who are stressed about the tests," Julie tells me. "The kids are okay with them. The teachers and the district staff are very focused on following standards and meeting performance goals. When I discuss computer activities with teachers, we often go to the district curriculum guide to ensure there is a match.

"The math lessons you just saw are aligned to the curriculum," Julie assures. "It is not busywork, but something that is relevant. It provides useful reinforcement to our curriculum."

She goes on to describe a recent off-site meeting. All of the school's specialists were there, including resource teachers for special-needs students; the gifted teacher; reading specialists; Julie herself; and the instructional resource teacher, who is responsible for ensuring that all activities are aligned to curriculum standards. They spent the day exploring how alignment can be accomplished. *The concepts are in place,* I think, *but does execution follow?*

▸ ▸ ▸

Julie and I walk to my last stop of the day: a 4th grade social studies classroom where I am to observe a curriculum-aligned, technology-supported history and geography lesson. Taped to each computer monitor is an overhead transparency showing an outline map of the state. Students trace the state's borders using a drawing program. Referring to a map in their textbook, they draw lines that define the state's several geographic regions. When printed, the maps will be part of a unit report—perhaps pointed to with pride as a creative outcome of technology use. Is this what billions have been spent to accomplish?

I have a final question for Julie before I leave the school. What one thing would make her more effective? Another coordinator, she tells me. The job is too big for one person. She receives good support from the district help desk, she says, adding, "My tech support person is absolutely wonderful. He takes time to explain to me. But I don't get much support on the content side."

That does not surprise me.

Viewpoint

Style over substance. Mechanics over meaning. These were the priorities I often observed in my school visits. Content was secondary; teacher and students focused on the *how*, not the *what*.

The earthquake activity at Lambert typified the problem I saw in so many schools. Clearly, classroom teacher Beth Anderson was not well-acquainted with Excel. I suppose she deserves a certain amount of credit for teaching the lesson herself rather than relying on Julie, the technology coordinator, to teach it. And perhaps she had no greater goal than to acquaint her class with some basic Excel functions. She did that and acknowledged that the school curriculum did not require Excel at 5th grade. Her lesson was preparation for required instruction at the 6th grade.

Technology advocates recommend that productivity tools be taught using relevant content, that the substance of the lesson should be relevant to the curriculum. Unfortunately, in Beth's class, and in many others I observed, the content was virtually ignored. Instead, the focus was almost exclusively on color, font selection, sound, animation, music selection, and other features. Content was not unlocked by the wise use of programs but imprisoned by the attention to mechanics.

I found the attention to mechanics especially troubling when PowerPoint was used. The PowerPoint presentations were highly prized by students, teachers, and parents—in fact, I learned that PowerPoint presentations have become something of a staple at parents' open houses. Parents who are unacquainted with PowerPoint can easily conclude that the flashy presentations reflect the skills of their sons or daughters when, in fact, most of the credit belongs to the software program itself.

Some teachers I met really believed that wrestling with the mechanics of PowerPoint helps students become intimately familiar with the content they were trying to present. One experienced principal convincingly maintained that PowerPoint and Web resources let students produce in-depth reports that would be impossible with traditional media (see Chapter 7). She was a very credible advocate for technology, but she spoke as the leader of a high-income school with small classes and an experienced and energetic technology coordinator. Unfortunately, her school was more the exception than the rule. If substance prevailed over style, was it because of this combination of leadership, resources, and purpose? I believe so.

►►► 16

Carter
Elementary School

I PULL INTO THE PARKING LOT OF CARTER ELEMENTARY SCHOOL at 8:30 a.m. The school is in northern California, in a neighborhood several miles from Harrison Elementary (see Chapter 11). Brand-new upper-middle-class homes with two- and three-car garages face one another across streets that seem strangely empty. Then I realize the California commuters must have left at least an hour ago, that preschool children are in day care, and that school-age kids are inside Carter Elementary or one of the private, Christian schools that serve the area.

The stillness is broken when I enter the school office. A 1st grade boy, looking feverish, sits in a chair while the school secretary tries to locate his mother. Two 5th or 6th grade girls, waiting patiently to deliver attendance information from their teacher, chat about a favorite boy band. A volunteer mother receives instructions from an administrative aide on how to operate the copy machine. Daily announcements come over the address system.

A young man with an intense and serious face walks out from behind the counter. "I'm Martin Davidson," he says. "Welcome to Carter. I hope I can be of help."

This is the vice principal with whom I have exchanged e-mails. Thanks to our message exchange, I know that he has been at Carter for a year and that he is in line for the principalship at a new school under construction within the rapidly growing district. Like Harrison Elementary (see Chapter 11), Carter is made up entirely of portable classrooms—36 of them.

"They give with one hand and take away with the other," Martin tells me, explaining that the primary grade classrooms in the new school will be smaller than the portables Carter is using. State law mandates that kindergarten through grade 3 classes have no more than 20 students. This makes the existing rooms very spacious, able to accommodate computers and the other interest centers around which many primary classes are organized.

Space, I am learning, is a precious commodity for teachers, particularly for those who use technology. "Kids need room," Martin says. "We've got it now, but we'll lose in the new school," he says as we walk out of the administrative building.

"Last year, only 12 of our computers were linked to the Internet. Those were in the 5th and 6th grade classrooms. This year, the 33 lab computers are connected, and we are connecting the 3rd and 4th grade rooms. It is very expensive because we have to dig cable trenches to extend lines to these portable buildings.

"Next year," he continues as we walk across an area between pods of portables, "the 1st and 2nd grades will probably be added, but it will be a waste of money unless the computers are upgraded. Some of them are old Apples and only a few are Internet compatible."

Where does money for the technology investment come from? Some comes from state allocations, Martin says, but a lot comes from grants, gifts, and fundraising. He describes how one parent, a sales representative for a technology program that nurtures aural discrimination, arranged a grant that allowed Carter to acquire the system. The parent gave Martin a filled-out grant request. All he had to do was sign it.

"That's the way things work. Hardware companies are always sending us filled-out grant requests or samples of successful proposals used by other schools. We just replace the other school's name with ours.

"Our parent organization raised $50,000 this year. Most of it will go to teacher salaries. Our tech coordinator's salary comes out of that. She's a parent who is interested in computers. She's not a certified teacher, but she does a good job. She's on a nine-month contract to work six hours a day. Unfortunately, she is off this term, so the teachers are on their own. Let's go into the lab to see what is going on."

▶ ▶ ▶

We enter a room that has 32 computers ringing its perimeter. In one corner is a teacher's desk. Above the desk hangs a 34-inch monitor that can show an enlarged picture of the teacher's computer screen. Today the monitor is blank. The 3rd grade teacher, who has brought her class for their assigned lab period, sits at a table in the middle of the room correcting a set of math worksheets.

"They're working on their math facts," says the teacher, nodding her head toward the students. She alternately corrects her papers and watches the computer screens.

The students are supposed to be working on a popular math game. The game helps them learn their facts, she tells me, but I notice that she speaks with little conviction or enthusiasm. The number of red marks on the papers she's correcting do not suggest that the program has been successful.

I walk around the classroom and observe what the students are doing. Many are slouching in front of their screens, talking quietly with classmates on either side, slowly fingering the keys, or clicking the mouse with little show of intensity or interest. As I come near, they straighten up, stare fixedly at the screen, and then just as quickly slouch down when they realize I'm just looking. They make little pretense of caring about the rockets that move haltingly across the screen while two-digit math problems pop up for them to answer. This is not PlayStation 2.

As we leave the portable classroom, Martin tells me that things are different when Bev Hughes, the lab aide, is here. Bev teaches whatever classroom teachers request, usually computer skills, such as how to use the mouse, save a file, or use the keyboard. She tries to tie her class to a topic the teacher is covering in the regular classroom.

Martin says he does not care for programs like the one we just saw. "I divide software into open-ended and close-ended. What we just saw was a close-ended program. I hate them. I much prefer open-ended programs that allow kids to find their own answers, that allow them to be creative.

"I came here to get technology going. A parent survey showed that technology is their number-one priority," he tells me. Martin suggests that I go on to some 5th and 6th grade classrooms by myself. Teachers know I am visiting the school and I'm wearing my sticker with a bright red apple and the word "Visitor" on it. He says he'll meet me in the teachers' lounge at the end of the morning.

► ► ►

For two hours, I walk in and out of classrooms. Teachers acknowledge me with a nod of the head as I quietly take a seat at the back or side of the room. Instruction is not interrupted, though the teacher often comes and chats easily while students work on activities, tests, or reading materials.

I feel welcome and enjoy just sitting and observing and listening. If technology is a priority for Carter parents, it does not seem one for the teachers. In half of the classrooms I visit, the computers are turned off. When they are on, half or fewer are in use. This is something I see repeatedly in my school visits: Almost without fail, at any given time, 80 percent of the classroom computers are not being used.

"To a fair degree, technology is overrated," one teacher tells me. "If you have books, books are just as good. I'm considered a techie, but I don't buy it all. Computers can help kids do more investigating through the Internet, but it can make them lazy, too. They go to a Web site and just cut and paste."

I hear similar caution at lunch when I ask teachers to tell me how they use technology:

• "Let's just say I'm not sure it's worth taking 20 minutes of class time to type a sentence."

• "Keyboards don't fit my 3rd graders' hands. I'm worried about establishing bad habits."

• "California has hit accountability so hard that technology has to take a back seat; everything is focused on tests."

• "The computers we have in our classrooms are so old I'm not going to take time to learn what I can do with them. I'll wait till we get new ones."

• "My kids spend lots of time at home on computers and games. I want them to have a book in front of them when they're here in school."

• "Three computers in a classroom are simply not enough for 32 kids. They are just a distraction to the other kids and more trouble than they are worth. They make classroom management a problem, too."

The teachers' reservations are punctuated by occasional enthusiasm:

• "I have two old Macs in my 1st grade classroom. I can still use them for number and letter recognition. I'm trying to get two parent volunteers to work with kids who need help. Computers support my teaching; they don't replace it."

• "Computers help kids at risk. Computers can be motivational. I don't mean games—I don't use games—but kids can do reports on computers that look very good. They can produce something they can take pride in."

• "Kids use the Internet for research, but their research is only as good as the work I do beforehand finding sites. Still, I think the computer is a strong motivating factor."

Interesting, I think, but I try to keep my mind on the question: *Does technology affect measurable results?* I'm swimming now in technology waters, but it is all kind of murky.

▶ ▶ ▶

I spend an afternoon period in the school yard with Vice Principal Martin Davidson as he watches over the students. A 1st grader runs over to tell Martin that a big boy said a bad word. A chubby little girl says that someone took her pencil and won't give it back.

Martin listens with concern, as though each child were the only person in the yard. He asks the boy, "You don't want to do that when you get big, do you?" The boy responds by shaking his head vigorously. No, he won't say bad words when he's big. To the little girl, Martin responds, "Let's think what we should do about that," and the two plan a course of action. Both children go away satisfied that an adult has listened.

Viewpoint

Looking back on Carter Elementary School, I remember Martin's commitment to technology and his gentle concern for children. I also remember his discussion about classroom size. My school visits confirmed that adequate space is an important criterion for successful computer use.

Classroom size in new schools is largely controlled by state funding formulas. In most states, the government supports local school construction according to a specified number of square feet per student (usually about 100 square feet per child). For example, if a school is being built for 600 students, the state formula will support a 60,000-square-foot building.

Computers, as currently designed, take up 130 to 140 square feet per student. This figure allows computers to be set up on tables, rather than on desks, and factors in the space needed for monitors, keyboards, mouse pads, cables, printers, scanners, projectors, and storage cabinets for headphones, extra mice, and other support materials. Students also need enough area surrounding the computer to do traditional paper-and-pencil work and spread out their textbooks or other classroom materials.

Most often, I saw classrooms in which three to six computers were awkwardly positioned in a corner, placed up against a wall, set on an island of tables, or installed in carrels with walls separating one student from another. I saw classrooms in which teachers rigged cardboard walls between computers. I saw many different attempts to house the towers, the monitors, and the rest of the hardware. Often square pegs were forced into round holes.

Computer technology was not designed to fit the schools inherited from the past, and yet new schools are not being built 30 to 40 percent larger to provide space for today's hardware. That hardware will shrink, but until it does, schools will continue to wrestle with the unsatisfactory makeshift solutions to the problem of space.

PART IV ◄◄◄

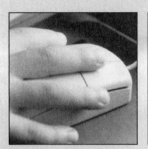

Too Troubled to Focus

The four schools in this section face serious problems, most of which were inherited from previous administrations or resulted from severe budget or societal challenges. As with the schools in Part III, I am not judging the districts' or schools' programs as a whole. Rather, I am reflecting on how technology is used in these schools and the related challenges that they must deal with. Technology cannot make a significant difference in student performance until administrative and budget problems are addressed. Only then will the focused use of technology have a substantive effect.

▶ ▶ ▶ *17*

Alexanderville
School District

I'M JOB SHADOWING TODAY, SEEING LIFE THROUGH THE EYES of Alexanderville School District's assistant technology coordinator, Bob Jacobson. Bob retired last spring after 30 years as a middle school language arts teacher. All of those years were spent in the Alexanderville School District. Now, he has returned to the district on a part-time contract in the technology department.

I am meeting Bob at the district technology office. As I swing off the interstate that rings this midwestern city, I pass reminders of Alexanderville's rural past. The occasional barn and farmhouse are interspersed with the plats of small, lower-income homes. These homes have pushed out from the neighboring city's urban core, radically altering the demographics of the school district.

Alexanderville's technology department occupies several classrooms on the third floor of a district administrative building, which for decades housed Alexanderville's high school. I enter a basement door and thread my way through a labyrinth of dimly lit corridors. I ascend a stairway to the second floor. Voices drift from several classrooms now used by the district's alternative high school program. I continue on the stairway to the third floor. At the top is a wall: The stairway leads nowhere. By day's end, I'll wonder if this is a metaphor.

► ► ►

I descend the stairs, locate steps at the opposite end of the hall, and make my way up to the technology office. Bob greets me and introduces me to Kevin Patterson, a technician with the district's technology support contractor, 21st Century Services.

Bob motions me to follow him, and we head to a classroom at the other end of the hall. Bob and Kevin are preparing it for an administrators' training class and they need to test the computer projector. "Administration comes first," Bob tells me as we enter the room. A tangle of wires snakes up from an electrical box in the middle of the room and continues along the floor and under two rows of tables.

Bright sun floods in from the east, making the shadeless room much too bright for a computer projector. We find an old piece of oilcloth and three cardboard boxes, drape the oilcloth over a horizontal rod, and then flatten the boxes and prop them as shields against the invading light. Bob and Kevin test a laptop with the projector, and a pale image appears on the screen. By noon, the sun will be overhead and the makeshift window covers might do their job.

Returning to Bob's classroom office, we see Kevin demonstrate how to dislodge the cover from a computer tower. With an open palm, he smacks the metal side, popping it off. Bob steadies another computer, smacks it, and pops its metal side off too.

"That's easy," Bob says.

► ► ►

I follow Bob downstairs, out of the building, and across a parking lot to a newer two-story building. This is the current high school. As we walk in, Bob nods to a security guard, indicating that I am okay. It's between classes and the halls are crowded. Students rush, lockers slam, and voices call out as we dodge our way through the traffic. It reminds me of Boston at rush hour.

As we thread our way through the chaos, Bob explains that he will be adding some refurbished PCs to the school's equipment roster. He's not happy about it. The district has more than 800 Macs and about 300 PCs. Virtually all of his tech time is spent on the PCs, Bob says, but the decision to migrate to PCs was made "upstairs."

"Mr. Jacobson!" a voice calls out in happy recognition. A beaming girl stops before us, puts her arms around Bob, and says, "I thought you retired." She then looks at me and says, "I just love him. He's the best teacher I ever had." She releases Bob and asks him, "Are you back?"

"Part-time," he answers, and she hurries away to class. "I taught her in middle school," Bob explains. "She is very bright."

We enter a classroom, which looks like a computer workroom or repair shop. Five students stand waiting, four boys and a girl. They were members of Bob's middle school computer club. Now in high school, they continue to provide essential support to the district's technology department. The boys wear the urban uniform: low-slung, baggy pants and oversized T-shirts. One wears a bandana; two of the others wear their hair tightly braided into cornrows. The girl, whom Bob introduces as "possibly the brightest student in the freshman class," wears a satin jacket sporting the school colors and lion mascot.

Bob is coordinating a complex computer purchase, exchange, and upgrade. He points to 20 computer towers sitting against the wall, explaining to the students and me, "These are used PCs that we bought from 21st Century for $550 each. We bought 100. Sixty are going to faculty. A few have already been distributed. We're going to clean these 20 now and add memory. Then we'll use the old faculty computers in a new math lab."

Bob opens a box on a table, takes out a memory card, lifts a computer to the table, and demonstrates how to remove the cover. Smack! It falls away. From inside, he picks out a ball of dust the size of a walnut. "I once found one as big as my fist," he tells me, then demonstrates to the students how to clean the computer's interior with a handheld vacuum.

He shows the watching students where the memory card goes and then says, "Okay, let's get started on the other 19."

"All today?" asks one of the boys in feigned protest.

"Would you prefer study hall?" Bob asks in turn, and the students begin lifting the computers to the tables. Bob explains that twice a week, Alexanderville High School has a 90-minute period called Lion Time that is set aside for assemblies, club meetings, or study hall. Bob's computer group is not a formal club, but the principal allows these students to work on technology projects during Lion Time, provided that they carry a signed authorization slip.

Today, one of the students doesn't have an authorization slip, so Bob has me follow him to the principal's office, where he confers with the secretary about getting the student a slip. From behind a closed door, we hear loud, impassioned voices. The secretary explains that there are two parents inside, so maybe Bob should come back at another time. He agrees.

As we start to leave, the secretary asks Bob whether he can show her how to alphabetize in their new version of Word. Bob gives a short lesson, and we head back to the workroom. On the way, Bob explains that the school network was attacked by a virus earlier in the fall, rendering it virtually unusable for three weeks.

"We had to clean and re-image each of our 1,150 computers, one at a time. That really set back plans to get our labs in order."

Bob goes on to explain that only one high school lab is operating, and it is just barely managing. The lone survivor is the business lab, with "a bunch of broken machines" overseen by a substitute teacher.

The old math lab, once supported by a pilot program sponsored by a nearby military base, was disassembled four years ago. Math instruction has suffered without it, Bob feels. Math teachers want a new lab soon. "I've learned to listen to those teachers who are enthusiastic," Bob tells me. "I try to do what they ask. The labs I've set up are what they want, not always what I think they should have. But I'd rather serve those committed to technology."

How many are committed? I ask. Fourteen out of 60, he answers.

Teachers don't feel a part of the technology decision-making process, Bob tells me. High-level administrators make decisions and expect teachers to implement the new technology. However, without teacher commitment, the technology doesn't really benefit anyone. He gives an example: "The district invested in a computer-based tutorial and remediation program. Teachers didn't buy into it, but they use it because it keeps kids quiet and offers the teachers a respite while kids sit and stare at the screen."

▸ ▸ ▸

Bob is working with a high school teacher to create a multimedia development lab. We walk back to the old building, where the lab will be located. Next to the technology office are two small rooms. It takes an active imagination to see these rooms as a high-tech lab. Parts of old computers and printers lie on the floor and counter. A broken ceramic table lamp sits atop an old breakfront cabinet. Behind its glass windows are more discarded computer parts.

"High-end graphics equipment will be hard to come by," Bob says, as he describes how he wants to equip the lab. "State technology funds are drying up. Two years ago, our technology budget was $2 million. This year it is $400,000. I can't guess what it might shrink to next year."

He goes on to say that supplies are an ever-increasing problem. The district bought two new ink-jet printers during the past year. Ink cartridges cost $50 each and are not budgeted by the district. If teachers want to use the printers, they must buy the cartridges themselves.

Bob recently inventoried printers in the district's middle school. He found only 25. One of these was subsequently ruined when a teacher fed a piece of heat-sensitive fax paper into it.

▸ ▸ ▸

Bob gets a cell phone call from a teacher of freshman English. We'll stop in her classroom on our way back to check on the students doing the upgrades. As we enter the room, I see students seated in three circles. They are discussing *To Kill a Mockingbird*. Several students sit alone working on homework.

The teacher explains that she has been unable to access the Internet. Bob begins to troubleshoot the problem while I sit down near a circle of desks to listen. The discussion among this group of students is lively. They don't seem to miss the computer.

Bob solves the access problem, and we go back to check on the upgrade project. Lion Time is just about over. All 19 computers have been cleaned and all 19 have new memory installed. The students have attached and checked out mice, keyboards, and monitors.

As Bob and the students put the computers back on the floor, I look through several math books on a shelf. Copyrights for the textbooks range from 1981 through 1984. At my feet are three tubs of manipulatives that accompany a newly adopted general math series. The shrink-wrap that covers them is unbroken.

▶ ▶ ▶

The bell rings, and the student helpers go off to their next class. Bob leads me to the home economics computer lab, from which he wants to borrow a computer. The home economics teacher became ill during the first week of school. Substitutes are handling her classes, and the lab is sitting unused. He pulls a large key ring from his pocket and searches for the right one. "I spend 10 percent of my day locking and unlocking doors," he tells me.

Bob props the door open. Across the hall sits a security guard. From the guard's location, he can see both ends of the hall, a stairwell, and two entrances. Bob asks whether the guard will watch the door while he carries the computer upstairs. The guard agrees, but says he can't stay there forever. He has other posts in the school.

Walking down the second-story corridor, we pass an open classroom. The teacher sees Bob and comes out of the classroom. "Is that my computer?" he asks.

The teacher says that one of Bob's student helpers took his computer several days ago. The student brought an upgraded computer in exchange, but it didn't have his grade book software. "I'm missing all my records," the teacher says. "I need them to issue quarter grades."

Bob promises he'll find the old computer but reminds the teacher that the software maker no longer supports the grade book program. "It works for me," the teacher says, insisting again that he can't issue grades without it.

As we walk away, Bob describes a dilemma the teachers face. The grade book program works on only a few of the high school's computers, yet the faculty handbook says teachers must use it.

This is not the only technology quandary that the district has faced. Two years ago in April, 21st Century Services' predecessor lost a bid for the contract to continue tech support for the district. They stopped working in early May, one month before the contract expired, and by the time 21st Century took over in midsummer, conditions had deteriorated. Four of the five high school labs were out of commission, general maintenance of Apple computers at the elementary and middle schools had lapsed, and high school and administrative PCs were riddled with viruses.

During that same year, a former district tech director invested several million dollars in a new Microsoft NT network. Its multiple servers were designed to support a new administrative software package. Scant attention was given to instructional needs. The administrative software was purchased and installed, but the tech director resigned before the program went live. Soon after, the district's newly appointed superintendent reviewed the administrative software plan, balked at the long-term cost, and killed the project.

▶ ▶ ▶

Back in the technology office, Bob takes a call from Rebecca Willis, a special education teacher at Fairacres Elementary School, one of the schools Bob supports. Rebecca is having a problem accessing student records from her reading motivation program.

Bob thinks he knows the problem. He is surprised that Rebecca cannot handle it, as he describes her as very computer savvy. Last year, Rebecca was one of two technology coaches at Fairacres. They had supplemental contracts and were responsible for helping teachers integrate technology into the curriculum. They also troubleshoot hardware and software problems. With budgets tight this year, the supplemental contracts were not renewed, but Rebecca has informally continued in that role. We head to Fairacres to meet with her.

"I believe in technology," Rebecca tells me when we meet. "If I didn't support it here, it wouldn't be used."

Rebecca has been teaching for 22 years. This year she has 5th and 6th grade special education students. Each of her 10 pupils has an IEP that she must update each quarter. Her computer, she says, makes this heavy administrative burden easier. It also helps her meet some instructional challenges.

"I want these kids to learn to type," she tells me. "The district has no typing program at this level, but I got a program to use with them. I have two electronic encyclopedias and an electronic dictionary. I help the students use them, but I teach them to use book versions as well."

I sense a lack of coordination between Rebecca's special ed curriculum and the general curriculum. She confirms it. The district adopted a new reading program last year, but no one ordered teacher editions for Rebecca. The year before, the district adopted a new science program; Rebecca did not receive a teacher edition for that program, either. The kicker, she says, is that each teacher edition came with support software and other materials that would have allowed her to align her special education instruction with the general curriculum. How much better might this handful of children have been served, I wonder, if Rebecca had been able to guide them using the curriculum-related support software?

Rebecca stresses that teachers need to be very familiar with the programs they assign to students: "Teachers use software, but they don't know what is on the disks. They don't have time to find out. They can't just tell students to use a program. Kids need the support of a teacher."

She doesn't think many teachers give that support at Fairacres. "If you look around," she says, "you'll probably find computers turned on in no more than 6 of the 30 classrooms here. In some of those, only the teacher's computer will be on."

As Bob and I walk through the halls to leave, I peer into each classroom. Rebecca's estimate was right.

Viewpoint

The visit to Alexanderville was a troubling experience. As I shadowed Bob and listened to teachers, I wondered who would want his job. The problems I saw appeared to be the legacy of past administrations. The district had a new superintendent, new principals had been assigned to several schools, and the technology staff were new. Despite an occasional tinge of cynicism, however, Bob was committed to the district and especially to its students. They loved him and he loved them. Why else would he leave retirement for a position that paid almost nothing?

The most upsetting aspect of Alexanderville was that so much had been spent and so little had trickled down to serve students and teachers. Was the problem poor administrative decisions made in the past, the shrinking budgets, or the innate complexity and immaturity of the technology? I sense that it was a mix of these, with the last being the core constraint.

This school, like many other districts, set lofty goals for its technology initiatives. I now believe that districts often aim higher than is realistic, given the administrative, financial, and technological resources they can commit. Technology has been and continues to be a moving target, as better, faster computers exceed those already in place and as the Web promises quicker, better, broader access to instruction and information resources. One solution to the problem of the mismatch between goals and resources may be to focus those resources on the few high-priority, high-return roles that I discuss in Chapter 22.

▶▶▶ 18

Porter
Elementary School

I SLIP QUIETLY INTO THE BASEMENT CLASSROOM. TWO 3RD grade boys lie on the carpeted floor. Chins propped in their hands, they look intently at a board on the carpet between them. The board is painted with a grid pattern of three-inch squares.

"It's just like adding," says Kevin, lying to the left of the board and looking at an array of short wire strands. Each strand holds eight azure-colored beads. On the right side of the board, Adam watches as Kevin extends his index finger, reaches out, and touches one strand of beads, then another, then another until he has fingered all eight.

"Sixty-four," Kevin tells Adam. "Eight 8s are 64."

"Now take eight away," says Adam. "Sixty-four, 63, 62," he counts down, touching each bead on one of the eight wires.

"Fifty-six!" shouts Adam. "It's like adding, then subtracting." His voice, like Kevin's, carries the excitement of discovery.

▶ ▶ ▶

The basement room is in the annex of Porter Elementary School, located in a midwestern city of 160,000. The annex was built in 1961; Porter's main building dates to 1891. In 1990, Porter became a Montessori magnet school as part of the district's desegregation plan.

Porter sits in the middle of a low-income urban neighborhood. Its single-family, wood-frame houses were built in the early 1900s and are home to second- and third-generation Appalachians who migrated north for World War II factory jobs. The hearts of many neighborhood residents remain in Kentucky, Tennessee, and West Virginia. Many of the jobs they came for have moved again—this time, south to Mexico or east to Asia.

Only some of Porter's students come from the neighborhood. Most are bused from throughout the district. Once plump with federal funds, the district ran up a $20 million deficit three years ago, which led to sharp spending cuts. The Montessori program's future is in doubt. In fact, doubt pervades almost everything at the school except Kevin and Adam's conviction that multiplication is like addition.

▶ ▶ ▶

Before I visited the 3rd grade classroom, I met with Principal Patty Harris. In her mid-40s, Patty has energy and good humor. With her job, she needs both.

"We were an all-Macintosh school," she tells me when I ask about the school's computer equipment. "Then last year the district moved to 100 percent PCs. A district tech coordinator talked us into going with Macs, and then he left the district, and I'm left holding the bag. I have a school full of computers that the district won't support."

The school has no computer lab, but Patty is trying to cobble one together: "As I get time, I'm trying to move Macs from classrooms into a lab. The Macs won't be networked, but they'll be in one place. If I get any money, I try to put new PCs in the classrooms. We have them in some of the rooms alongside the Macs. I'm also trying to get the district to send me computers from Ridgewood and Wilson, which closed last year. I've been able to find some PCs, but it may be too late to get many more. I have a paraprofessional who can run the lab. We'll just have to wait and see.

"Of course it's more than just getting the PCs. We need the software too. Teachers like their Mac programs. They want those same programs on PCs, so we need to buy new CDs or licenses. Some of the programs only come in the Mac format. We don't have much money for anything," she tells me.

"When PC versions exist and I can find money, it takes forever to get them running. If we want the programs on the network, the district tech office has to mount them. Our needs aren't high on their list. I'm between a rock and a hard place. I can't move broken Macs to the lab because I can't get them fixed. Teachers who use Macs in their classrooms don't want to lose them. We have Macs sitting next to PCs. That can be confusing for the kids, not to mention the teachers."

Patty gets up and motions me to follow. "Let me show you what we're up against," she says.

► ► ►

Porter's ceilings soar 12 feet overhead. Voices echo from six classroom doors that empty into the main hallway. We leave the old building, cross to the annex, and enter a first-floor classroom. It is empty except for Olive Johnson. Olive, Patty tells me, is her right hand—and left hand—in the school. Officially, Olive is the technology coordinator but she often serves as Patty's alter ego.

Patty asks Olive to describe some of Porter's technology challenges, then leaves. Olive needs no additional urging. During this free period, she is loading a popular early reading program on one of the school's new PCs.

"This is very time-consuming," Olive tells me. "I have to do it one computer at a time, and time is limited. I have only this one free period. My goal is to get our PCs to where the Macs were, but that is a long way off."

To complicate the shift to PCs, the district recently changed servers and server names. Internal addresses had to be changed, an imperfect procedure during times of such great flux. The used PCs that the school purchased must now be re-imaged, their software replaced; district support staff handles this task. However, because the budget crisis has reduced that staff, the re-imaging moves forward haltingly.

Olive explains that the district adopted a new reading program last year. It came with software that she and others want to use. "We mounted it on a few computers," she says, "but I don't have time to put it on my own.

"There was one reading support program I relied on. I used Title I funds to buy it. I can't afford to buy the PC version. I guess I'll just have to get along without it," she laments.

Before I can ask a question, 5th grade teacher Marie Oster comes in. "How am I supposed to use that thing?" she asks. Her tone is edgy, hostile. "That thing" is a new PC with an Internet hookup.

"They came and drilled a hole in my wall one day, they put wires in the next," Marie says. "I used the name you gave me to get access, but it doesn't work. I'm getting sick and tired."

Message delivered, Marie turns and leaves. Olive raises an eyebrow diplomatically, gives a barely visible shrug of her shoulder, and answers a question I have: Does the school see any benefits from the parent loan program?

Two years ago, the district bought the services of an Internet portal. As part of the service, 20 video game machines are made available to Porter. They come loaded with educational software that supports the new reading program. Parents can borrow them if they agree to spend half an hour three times a week playing it with their child.

"I don't have any way to measure the loan program's value," Olive says. "Maybe half of the parents use it, but I don't know."

► ► ►

Olive's reading class arrives. She gets up from the computer as a dozen children file in. Eight of them take places at two tables, and four gather at a table with Olive. All know the routine. The four children with Olive read in turn from their basal textbook. The other eight read silently from colorful paperbacks. Additional children from the class are with special-needs teachers or aides. They will rejoin their class later for more traditional Montessori activities.

It is common for classes to divide in this way throughout the school day. There is an amoebic character to the blending, dividing, and reblending that goes on in all schools, especially in a school like Porter, where a number of children qualify for special services and where enrollment turnover is high. Managing class makeup is a complex administrative procedure that complicates computer-based record keeping and undermines the use of computer management systems.

Many management systems that accompany software programs assume a classroom organization in which a stable group of children learns under the direction of a single teacher. That organizational model suits the constraints of software and may reflect the experience of the software developers, but it does not reflect the current reality of many classrooms—especially not in the lower elementary grades.

► ► ►

I meet that reality when I visit Porter's special education classroom. Twelve students sit individually or in pairs. The special ed teacher, Roberta Koughlin, and an aide work with students one-on-one. A computer is turned on, but sits unused while the children focus on worksheets or read books.

These children have been pulled out of their regular classes for special attention. Roberta speaks harshly to a 3rd grader who had fought with a classmate earlier in the morning. Her disciplinary message is delivered, her tone softens, and she asks gently, "How should you handle this in the future?"

"With words first," the boy answers. He walks to a seat and begins a worksheet.

Roberta motions to me to join her at the computer, where she proceeds to offer a rapid-fire catalog of comments about technology:

• "I use the CD-ROM story summaries that accompany our basal reading program. I use them to introduce stories and provide background and context. These children need that."

- "Look at this database I've developed. It includes everything I know about each child. I have to have that information ready for the main office. I can use it for developing and maintaining my IEPs. I don't use an electronic grade book because grade-book software can't handle all the information I have."

- "This reading software program is great, but labor-intensive. It requires full-time monitoring when the students use it. If the teacher is not keeping track, the kids just play."

- "Here at Porter, we have eight computers that go home to low-income families. The families get to keep them for six weeks. But the computers can't go to my IEP students because that would be seen as double dipping."

Roberta pauses, then calls to one of her students. "Come here, Wilbur and tell Mr. Pflaum what you can do."

Wilbur, a 3rd grader, approaches and struggles to say, "I wrote cursive." He returns to his seat, and Roberta quietly tells me that the district's occupational therapist advised her and Wilbur's parents that he would never learn to write; his small muscle and hand-eye coordination was too stunted. In Roberta's class, however, Wilbur has learned to type letters, then words, then sentences. Now, with higher confidence, a great deal of effort, and Roberta's careful guidance, he can write sentences in cursive.

"I have another student who has no use of his right arm and hand. We're helping his mother get funding for a home computer. Then we will teach him to type with his left hand. I think it will work.

"A computer can be a toy or a tool, depending on how it is monitored. Computers have to be monitored," she continues.

"This is a great program, but we only have the Apple version. When the Apples go away we won't have it anymore. We can't afford the PC version."

I ask my standard question: Do computers help increase measurable growth on proficiency tests? "Computers are a help in life," Roberta answers. "School today isn't about life, it's about proficiencies."

► ► ►

The bell for early lunch rings, and the children return to their regular rooms. I move to a 5th grade class that has late lunch. The room is organized into six centers. The computer center is against the wall just inside and to the left of the classroom door. It has one Macintosh and two PCs. An aide works with a student on a PC. She has an Excel spreadsheet open and is working on an activity to teach the concept of coordinates.

The teacher here is Linda Adkins; she's also a part-time technology coordinator. Linda is taking an evening course in computer-based instruction at the local state university. She learned about the coordinate activity in that course and plans to report back on how it worked with her students.

From what I observe, she will not report success. The aide struggles with Excel and the student looks on passively, confused. Finally, the aide shows the young girl how to save the spreadsheet to the desktop. There is no established file structure on the computer and no network connection for central server archiving.

Later, at the day's end, I revisit Principal Patty Harris. "See what a mess we have?" she asks. "It's like we're starting over. Last year we scheduled every child for computer time. That's just not possible now." With the challenges faced by Porter, I wonder how serious a loss that is.

Viewpoint

Porter Elementary faced a long list of challenges, including the community's low socioeconomic status, the system's budget crisis, the midstream shift from Apples to PCs, and the age of the school building. All contributed to Porter's difficulties.

Principal Patty Harris acknowledged that the Montessori program had been diluted by the emphasis on proficiencies and had also suffered from the district's practice of assigning new students to the school in the upper grades. These students, unaccustomed to the self-direction that a Montessori program assumes, often had trouble adjusting. The program, consequently, was adjusted to them. Nonetheless, the school had strong parental support, and Patty and her staff strove to incorporate computers in a way that supported the Montessori approach.

A core problem, I believe, is the complexity and immaturity of computer technology. Computer systems are not yet simple or transparent enough to work cost-efficiently in schools. They deliver important benefits, but increased test scores may not be one of them, and even the benefits they do provide may not equal their costs. With school budgets so tight, I doubt that technology, with its ambiguous impact on measured performance, will be budgeted at the levels seen during the past decade.

Newer, simpler, less expensive technologies will come, but they will not be adopted quickly by schools. Wireless technologies, notepad computers, and cheaper and larger memory systems all promise to simplify and drop costs. But schools will move slowly to them. School and district staffs have made financial and emotional commitments to current technologies that will make it very difficult to transition to new systems. Shrinking budgets will undoubtedly also hobble future transitions.

►►► 19

Fisher
High School

FISHER HIGH SCHOOL, ACROSS TOWN FROM PORTER ELEMENTARY, is also affected by the district's budget problems. Here, for example, is the status of the school's computer labs:

• Aerospace lab—Program suspended for lack of funds; computers now used for language arts classes.

• Law lab—Program suspended when the grant ran out.

• Engineering lab—Program suspended when the grant ran out.

• Math lab—Not running yet this year; technological conflicts between new math software and school's security software are unresolved.

• Computer skills lab—In use, teaching PowerPoint, Excel, Word, and keyboarding.

• Distance learning lab—Not in use; the French teacher who used it in previous years moved to another school.

- Medical technology lab—Program suspended, used for study hall and biology lab.

- Proficiency test prep labs—Two labs in use, one prepping for state science test, one for the state reading test.

The situation appears grim, but Fisher's principal is buoyant when we meet in his office on a hot August day. Classes at Fisher, which operates on a year-round calendar, are past the midterm point. Except for the sound of fans slicing at the humid air, the halls are strangely quiet as I make my way to the office. *There must be students here,* I think. *The parking lot is full of cars!*

Principal Austin Langley's office walls are covered in pictures of the school's football team. It's appropriate for a principal who speaks with the enthusiasm of a coach ready for the league championship.

"We're not the technology magnet, but we have a lot of technology. We have an academic curriculum organized around career clusters. Let me show you the school," he says, getting up from his desk and moving toward the door.

I follow, and Austin introduces me to Margaret Adams, a trim, white-haired woman in her 50s. Quickly, he explains who I am and asks her to tell me about Fisher's technology, then bring me to the library. A two-way radio buzzes. Austin unhooks it from his belt and turns back toward his office, listening as he walks.

Margaret is one of Fisher's three technology coordinators, all of whom are working on a supplemental contract. She seems uncertain of what she should say, but starts telling me about the school's labs. Until recently, grants drove the school's technology programs. Federal and state money cascaded into Fisher. But when the district hit a budget crisis, most of the programs could not be sustained. Staff were trimmed, central office support diminished, doors were locked, and computers were unplugged or rechanneled to other uses.

Margaret and I walk into the hall, heading to the library. "We received 72 computers from the state program," she says. "We have between 45 and 50 teachers, so every teacher got one. The computers are attached to scan converters so they can display on the class TV monitors. Maybe 15 of the teachers use them. Some of the TVs don't work."

I look up at a hallway clock. It reads 7:05. My watch reads 9:10. We head upstairs toward the library. At the top of the stairs, a second hallway clock reads 3:15.

▶ ▶ ▶

In the library, three students stand at the librarian's desk. One is signing a register, one is sullen and silent, and the third talks with the librarian, Sara Carter. Sara is young, well dressed, businesslike, and tired. She rifles through a file of papers, exclaims, "Here it is," and nods her permission to the 15-year-old boy in front of her, tipping her head toward a table of computers in the middle of the room.

"I spend half my day on authorizations," she tells me after we've been introduced and Margaret departs. "I sign in every student and check to see that we have a signed Authorized Use Policy statement on file. If parents and students haven't signed one, the kids can't use the computers. I'm more of a security guard than a librarian."

Why, I wonder, don't the students have accounts and passwords?

"It's a matter of dollars," she replies. "We have one password for the library, and I have to enter it for each student." She walks from her desk to where the just-approved student is sitting, opens a dialog box, enters a password as he looks on, then returns to the waiting students. The line has grown to four.

While Sara continues to check authorizations, I walk around, looking over students' shoulders. On screens I see Web sites for Yahoo, MTV, *People* magazine, and Encarta. Several students type in Word. A girl snaps her fingers, rocking back and forth in her chair, headphones wrapped around her head.

Fifteen minutes later, when Sara can once more give me her attention, I ask her how she compares the quality of research students do on computers with research they do using traditional print materials.

"With the computers, students cut, paste, and plagiarize," she answers. "They don't really read. They look for video clips and graphics. We don't have money for programs that scan for plagia-rized material. When we had magnet funds, we got whatever we wanted. But now, we don't even have a technology budget. It's a problem to keep up and replace old and broken equipment. And we only have three teachers on part-time contracts to support tech-nology integration. We—"

Sara breaks off as a bell rings. Students at computers start shut-ting down, new students come in the door, and she returns to the desk. She shrugs her shoulders toward me with an apologetic ges-ture, checks the next name on the register, and once again begins to leaf through the stack of Authorized Use Policies.

► ► ►

I head for the education lab, set up to help students explore careers in teaching. A uniformed security guard stands at the bottom of the steps, staring emotionlessly as students move up and down the cor-ridor. Despite the crowd, the hallways strike me as strangely quiet—not what I expect of high school today nor what I remember of high school in the 1950s—not even what I saw at Longworth High two weeks ago. It is not the quiet of self-discipline and order. It seems more the quiet of despair.

I find the education lab and its teacher, Natalie Saunders. She stands behind a student, waving me to join her. I count the students. There are 18: 13 girls and 5 boys.

"We are watching a 10-video series on issues in teaching. We are on the sixth," Natalie explains. "The series is about how to handle discipline problems. These students get practical experience because part of the class involves tutoring at the Burnett and Carlyle Schools' day care centers."

She goes on to describe how the students watch a video, take notes, and write an essay on what they saw and heard. They next develop PowerPoint presentations based upon the essays. She asks three students to review their presentations with me.

Each presentation makes heavy use of PowerPoint graphics. Let-ters and words slide from left to right; they fade in and out; they drop down from the top and disappear off the bottom of the screen.

Sentences build one word at a time. Colors change. Music pours out, then drains away. The presentation copy repeats verbatim words and phrases I have seen earlier on the video monitor. Two of the three essays are not really essays but outlines. The essays may come later, or not at all. Now it is all about PowerPoint, music, and words that move.

"Keep these presentations," Natalie advises the students. "You'll need PowerPoint resumes for college admission. Keep these templates and use them then." The bell rings, signaling that it is time for me to go to an honors English class.

▶ ▶ ▶

The hallways are a little more animated now, perhaps because it is the first lunch period. A boy darts past me, hooks his arm around a stair rail, and hurtles himself up the staircase. He is closely followed by another, faster boy who grabs him at the top of the stairs, gets him in a headlock, then laughs and loosens his grip. They walk away chatting. Their horseplay is laced with obscenities.

Thirteen students are in the honors English class. The teacher is Margaret Adams, whom I met earlier. Part of Margaret's supplemental technology coordinator job is to nurture and support other teachers who want to integrate technology into their classes. Today, she is nurturing the PowerPoint skills of her advanced English students. Each has built a presentation about a college or university that interests them. There will be seven presentations today.

As the students set up the digital projector, I talk with their teacher. When I ask if the use of technology at Fisher has led to measurable performance improvements, Margaret responds that it hasn't and that the problem is poor teacher-training. "Teachers don't use technology because they don't know how to," she says. "The district service center offers some very good classes, but they are after school. Who wants to drive there to take a class after a day of teaching?"

I ask about online professional development courses. Do teachers at Fisher take them? "No," she replies. "The district doesn't give us time during the day. Teachers aren't going to do it after school or at home. The district has to give us released time during school hours. If the district made technology a priority, teachers would too. Right now only a handful of teachers use computers. I could count them on these fingers," she says, holding up her hand with fingers spread apart.

The projector is working and the first presentation begins. I settle into a chair at the side. The computer balks and PowerPoint freezes on the opening screen.

"I'll just use my color printouts," the student presenter tells us. She takes a sheath of color prints, holds up the first one, and reads it aloud. It's the name and shield of a southern state college. In sequence, we see the campus map, the college motto, and a chart showing how the departments are organized, all cut and pasted from the school's Web site.

The PowerPoint software works for the second presentation. Rock music plays loudly as one slide fades into another, each cut and pasted from the Web site of a private college in Detroit. No commentary accompanies the slides. Margaret urges students to critique the presentations.

"The music keeps you focused," a voice calls out.

Another voice, little more than a whisper, says, "Cut and paste."

"Go on," Margaret says, and the third presentation begins. More rock music, more copy and graphics from a school's Web site, this one the University of Southern California.

"Cut and paste," the voice whispers again.

Margaret looks annoyed and tells the next two students to be ready. The whispering has stopped, but it rings in my mind. *Cut and paste,* I think, as borrowed screens from two state university sites follow one another with only slight edits.

The sixth presentation is by a girl who has applied to the engineering program at a state university. She has organized her own ideas and tells about the school in her own words. The pictures and graphics are clean, direct, and uncluttered.

Number seven is back to cut and paste.

"I am amazed at what they can do," Margaret says, as the students shut down the computer and projector. "I would not have guessed they could do this. I'm also having them write essays based on the presentations and their research."

I tell her that I am amazed, too.

► ► ►

After thanking Margaret for letting me sit in, I find my way to Ron Anderson's classroom. Ron teaches geometry and this is his free lunch period. He sits eating a sandwich in the empty room. Ron has taught math at Fisher for more than 20 years. The math lab adjoins his classroom. He'll use it, he says, as soon as he can solve some difficulties with a new algebra software system. He calls it a system because the program comes on CD-ROMs but has links to the publisher's Web site. The system has encountered conflicts with the school's security program.

"I'll get it figured out," Ron says, "but it's taking a lot of time. I'm pretty much on my own. The district makes sure I have the proper licenses, but they leave it to me to get it running. I understand that, but it takes time."

I ask him my question about technology's effect on measurable performance.

"Let me put it this way," he says. "Without technology, we'd be a lot further behind. Its role in boosting scores may not be apparent because kids coming up know less. Technology may be helping to fill the gap. Kids today just get passed on without acquiring skills. Face it, elementary teachers are teachers of reading. They teach what they are comfortable with, and they are not comfortable with math.

"Also," he continues, "kids today have a very low frustration level. They want instant gratification, instant response. They get frustrated with the printed page. Computers don't frustrate them as much."

Ron tells me that he uses technology as a tool for himself and for instruction. He keeps his grades on an Excel spreadsheet that "makes life a whole lot easier." He recently selected a new calculus textbook and expects to use its accompanying software for demonstrations. His geometry class will start in a half hour, and he invites me back for it. He won't be using technology, but I am interested in observing.

I take the time to walk through Fisher's halls. About half the classes are in session, the other half at lunch. As I pass filled classrooms, I look in through open doors or windows. No computers are being used, but I see two teachers at overhead projectors.

By the time I return to Ron's classroom, things are underway. There are 23 students in the class. Eighteen sit in student chairs facing a whiteboard at the front of the classroom. Two sit at a large table in the back of the room. On it are three computers that are not operating. To the right, three students sit at a second table. One has his head down on the table, sleeping. Two of the students in chairs also rest their heads on their desks, eyes closed.

Ron holds a copy of the previous evening's homework, which was preparation for tomorrow's test. He and the students go through the problems one by one. A girl named Diamond challenges him on several questions that she missed. She is brash, outspoken.

"I couldn't have done that wrong," she protests. "You sure you know this?"

Diamond knows where she went wrong, and it is apparent she understands the content. Her banter with Ron is good-natured, edging toward disrespect, but it's obvious to me that there is a real rapport between Ron, Diamond, and the dozen or so students who join the conversation.

The students in the class are either 9th or 12th graders. The 9th graders are bright students who did well in 8th grade algebra. Many of the 12th graders have failed an earlier math class and need this course to graduate.

With the review finished, Ron says they will spend the balance of the period on a new topic, complementary angles. On the whiteboard, he starts to draw a set of linear pairs. There is protest, led by Diamond. It's not fair, they say, to start a new topic before tomorrow's test. They want to use the rest of the period to study.

Ron continues to draw. With simple, precise lines he shows complementary pairs, supplemental angles, and vertical angles. He then begins a lucid explanation, asking questions and eliciting answers.

Students come to the whiteboard and offer explanations of the geometric principles. The number of engaged students has increased from 12 to 15 or 16. One who was sleeping rouses and joins in. I follow the discussion and solve the problems, sometimes ahead of the students, sometimes behind. Diamond always beats me.

After 20 minutes, the bell rings. Students gather their backpacks while discussion continues. As the classroom empties, I approach Ron and ask him about Diamond. "Is she as bright as she seems?" I ask. "Why is she in this class?"

"She is here because I flunked her last year," he tells me. "She wouldn't do the work and I don't just pass students on. It makes me feel good that she's making it the second time around."

My next class is next door. As I leave the room, I wonder whether Ron would be a more effective teacher with a computer instead of a whiteboard. Would one of those students whose head never left the table or desk have been awakened by technology?

▶ ▶ ▶

Before I can answer the question, I run into Principal Austin Langley again. He has come to show me the test-prep class I'm about to enter.

"Students have to pass a 9th grade state proficiency test in science to graduate," he says. "We assign this class to seniors who haven't passed it. No one is exempt unless a parent signs a waiver and takes responsibility for the child's performance.

"We have two test-prep classrooms. Next door, we teach reading each semester. Here, we prep for the science test one semester, for the social studies the other. We're prepping for science now."

About 20 students sit at desks arranged in a semicircle and facing a screen at one end of the classroom. A girl reads aloud from the state's science test-prep book. The passage, which describes pond life, is followed by multiple-choice questions. The girl reads fluently and flawlessly. Students in turn give answers to the questions, debating which answer is correct and why.

"When are we going to use the computers?" a boy asks the teacher, referring to the machines that line the room's perimeter. I understand from the principal that the computers are loaded with test-prep programs designed specifically for this state.

"I don't think we can," the teacher replies. "They've been frozen all morning. They're just not working. We'll watch a video instead." The class groans as a projector starts a 20-minute video on the water cycle.

I decide to skip this and head for the medical technology lab, where five students sit at computers. They talk loudly with one another, giving little attention to monitors or keyboards. The talk is not about school.

At the teacher's desk sits a middle-aged man. I introduce myself and learn that he's a substitute and that this is a class in business law. The five students in the lab are all that are left after the rest drifted away with passes to the library or bathroom. He allows the remaining students to do their homework.

The substitute is a graduate student working on his master's degree at the local state university. He substitute teaches when he can. "The problem with these kids is that they are not motivated," he volunteers. "Kids want the benefits of an education without the hard work. Their parents don't encourage them because they don't understand the dynamics of a knowledge-based technological society.

"Their parents or grandparents came here to work in the car plants. When times are good, they make a lot of money. They did it without an education. Why do their kids need one? They don't know the world has changed—Sit down and be quiet!" he interrupts himself, as he shouts for the attention of a girl who has left her computer and is tousling the hair of a boy at an adjoining table. The girl returns to the computer and stares defiantly at the screen, hands folded in front of her. Neither she nor the computer speak.

Viewpoint

It's easy to spot the victims at Fisher High School: the students. I wish I could find the villain. Candidates include the superintendent and school board who spent beyond their means and then had to cut drastically; teachers who praised accomplishment that was mediocre at best; a substitute teacher who collected a check, didn't teach, and performed poorly as a child sitter; and students who slept through class, throwing away their opportunity to learn.

There were heroes at Fisher, too: Teacher Ron Anderson, who set standards and inspired many students to meet them; Diamond, who woke up soon enough to use her innate strength and intelligence; the aspiring engineering student who didn't cut and paste when cutting and pasting was not only tolerated but rewarded.

But categories like villain, victim, and hero are too clear cut. Once again, Fisher showed that school technology use is about shades of gray. Once again, I encountered a disturbing overuse of PowerPoint and the familiar obsession with mechanics over meaning. But then once again, I saw brighter possibilities—this time, the work of that future engineer who created a presentation with care and reflection while those around her were satisfied to cut and paste. The choice is not is to reject technology or embrace it, but to use it with thought and discrimination.

►►► 20

Lincoln
Elementary School

"YOU TAKE THAT GROUP," 1ST GRADE TEACHER LOUELLA JACKSON tells me, pointing to a table in the center of the classroom where two boys and two girls are seated. "They're working on short *i* words. José is the leader. He knows what to do. See that they keep working."

LouElla speaks with authority. It is a voice I recognize—a voice like my own 1st grade teacher's. But that is where the similarity ends. My teacher wore a nun's habit; LouElla wears blue jeans and a green knit shirt embroidered with the words "Lincoln Elementary School." I am here to observe, but LouElla has turned me into an aide. She needs help and I will do.

My planned 45-minute visit stretches past midmorning. LouElla's class of 19 is divided among 5 activity centers. At 20-minute intervals, students move from one center to another. As I look on, children sort cards with pictures and short-vowel words. Three groups come to my table. They know the routine. If uncertain, a student team leader tells them what to do. I am less of an aide and more of a traffic cop as the kids move from station to station.

LouElla works with reading groups at the front of the class. The ringing of her classroom phone interrupts her four times; three times, she holds brief conversations as the students look on. Once she stretches the phone cord out the door, asking me to take charge while she talks in the hall.

There are seven computers set up against the wall in the back of the classroom. Four are being used by students working with a drill-and-practice program. They seem comfortable as they move and click the mouse, but after several minutes, their interest flags. The computer users fidget in their chairs, look around at the other groups, crane their necks to see the screen next to them, and talk with one another. Occasionally LouElla says, "Get to work back there," and they refocus on their screens for a little while.

With 20 minutes left in the class, LouElla tells my group to get their reading books. She comes to where I am and says quietly, "This is Serena's second day. She can't read and speaks very little English. Just let her look at the pictures."

Serena opens her book and looks at me with a shy smile. Then she starts to read, aloud and in English.

▶ ▶ ▶

It is easy to understand why LouElla was mistaken about Serena's skill level. At Lincoln Elementary, kids come and go constantly. Turnover is 70 percent a year. Principal turnover is also a problem. Principal Arlene Simmons, who met with me before class this morning, is the eighth principal in 11 years.

Lincoln Elementary is an inner-city school in a mid-Atlantic town of 100,000. It has more than 700 students. Of these, 65 percent are Latino, 22 percent black, and 35 percent non-English speaking. Many are recent arrivals from countries of the former Soviet Union. Ethnic tensions in the community have spilled over into school politics, with parents pressuring for the hiring of administrators and teachers from their own ethnic group. What's more, according to Lincoln's principal, many of the children come to the school "simply not ready to learn." For this reason, the school has invested in a pre-K consultant and many other support services.

When I spoke with Arlene early in the morning, our brief conversation was interrupted three times. Once, an aide brought her two girls who had been playing in the bathroom. Arlene referred them to the assistant principal. A father who had not sent his son to school regularly came to reenroll the boy. Arlene emphasized the importance of having the child in school each day. The father nodded his assent, but I suspected that the son would miss more days. A recently immigrated Latina mother came to enroll her son for the first time.

From Arlene, I learned that Lincoln has worked hard to address the multiple language needs of its population. Fifteen teachers have master's degrees in English as a second language (ESL). Three teach ESL exclusively.

Community health and welfare needs are also addressed. One school nurse works full-time and a second comes three days a week; a nurse practitioner is here twice a week. A doctor visits once a week, and there is an on-site child and family welfare worker, a full-time social worker, two children and youth caseworkers, a preschool consultant who helps families locate pre-K services, a full-time guidance counselor, three guidance interns who work 20 hours a week, and a school psychologist who works a four-day week.

Extra academic support comes from a reading specialist, three full-time paraprofessionals, and five Title I reading assistants. But no room has been made on the roster for a full-time technology coordinator. Technology coordination, defined as scheduling the computer lab and calling the district technology office when the network goes down, is a part-time responsibility of the media center director. There are slightly more than 300 networked, Internet-equipped computers in the school, nearly one for every two students. Most have been purchased with federal funds or through state-administered grants.

The school uses instructional software mandated by the district. It is an integrated learning system that prescribes activities and tracks individual performance. Each student is required to work on it 30 minutes a day—15 minutes on reading and 15 on math. The program is mounted on the district's server so that each teacher's use can be monitored.

▸ ▸ ▸

It's just after lunch and I am watching this program in a 5th grade classroom. Seven students sit before computers at a rectangular table. An eighth computer sits on the table unused. There is a ninth on the teacher's desk and a tenth on a table at the far end of the room.

Two large posters hang over the chalkboard. One reads, "Reading: MSD 4.5.2—Inferring, concluding, or generalizing about text evidence and experience." The other reads, "Mathematics: MSD 4.6.3—Using charts and graphs to represent data in social studies or science."

"Those are the standards we're covering today," says Heather McCarthy, the 5th grade teacher. "We're an underperforming school, so everything is very controlled by the district. We could be taken over by the state if we don't meet our improvement goals."

As Heather talks to me, a student teacher begins a math lesson at the front of the room. Heather is in her late 20s; the student teacher is in her 40s. She holds a spiral-bound teacher's edition of a textbook and addresses the 20 or so students who are not at computers. The lesson covers how to represent statistics with charts and graphs. The students at the computers alternately glance toward the front of the class, look at the screens before them, yawn with after-lunch sleepiness, or just sit.

A bee flies in the window, open to an unusually warm October afternoon. There is momentary chaos as excited children dodge or slap at the bee, shouting as the intruder comes near them. "Believe me, ladies and gentlemen," Heather calls out, "none of you is sweet enough for that bee to want to sting you." The children laugh, a firm whack with a book disposes of the bee, and quiet returns.

I stand behind several students at computers and watch as they hunt and peck or click to find an appropriate answer. The content covered by the program is simple geometry of the triangle. A boy has a multiple-choice problem on angles. Answer choices are *A, B,*

C, and *D.* He tries *A.* Wrong. Then *B.* Wrong, the computer tells him, the answer is *D.* Next problem. He tries *A.* Wrong. Then *B.* Correct. Next problem. He tries *A.* Wrong. Then *B.* Wrong.

"Sit up and try, Armando," Heather says to the boy I have been observing. She shakes her head at me in a gesture of mixed helplessness and understanding.

"I think the math is better than the reading," she tells me, referring to the software system. "I usually have time for only one subject, so if I have to make a choice, they do the math."

"Does it help them?" I ask.

"It might," Heather replies, "but we have so much to fit in that I have to make choices. If something goes, it is usually the computer. I'm supposed to sign up for one lab period a week, but when it's a choice between our test-prep books or the computer lab, I do the test prep."

I ask her how the students at the computers are going to learn the chart and graph content now being covered by the student teacher. Heather is not worried. I'm not sure whether this is a sign of confidence or despair.

"We just can't get everything done," she sighs. "Each day we are supposed to have two hours of reading and language arts, one hour of math, plus social studies, science, computers, an hour of test-prep a week, art, music, and constant testing. Each week we give tests for reading and math covering the proficiencies we taught that week. Three times a year we have Title I testing. And we seldom have enough time to cover the content we have to teach. We had only four days allocated to teaching long division!"

Heather looks at her watch and announces that it's time for the Pledge of Allegiance assembly. The entire school is meeting in the gym as part of a nationwide Pledge of Allegiance observance. She tells the student teacher to get the class organized while she accompanies me to the gym.

▸ ▸ ▸

As we leave the classroom, Heather is stopped by Kevin Miller, a 3rd grade teacher. He is intense, distressed. It is quickly evident that

Heather is a go-to person in the school. Kevin is extremely upset because a boy who missed 86 days last year in 2nd grade was promoted to his class. "It is another example of just pushing kids on," Kevin frets. "He's just not ready for this work."

Heather commiserates briefly, then walks with me to the gym. She leaves me at the back of the balcony, and I look down as classes file in. The horseshoe-shaped balcony is filling too. At the far end of the gym, an American flag stretches horizontally across the stage. I see children who've recently come from Mexico, El Salvador, Cambodia, Vietnam, Bosnia, and Haiti, as well as others whose families once came from Italy or Africa. The students stand with their hands over their hearts. They follow the principal as she leads them in the Pledge of Allegiance.

Viewpoint

I observed several allegiances at Lincoln. One was to our flag and to our country's values, which the school worked to imbue in the students, many of whom had only recently arrived here. Another was Arlene and her staff's allegiance to the students. When we met that morning, Arlene talked about the challenges at Lincoln, including 70 percent annual student turnover, intense medical and social service needs, and 95 percent of students qualifying for free or reduced-cost lunch. The answer, Arlene said, is not in computers. They can be an aid, she told me, "but nothing can replace a teacher."

Looking back, I'm struck by the contrast between Lincoln and Longfellow, the high-income elementary school along the New England coast (see Chapter 7). Both had substantial technological resources. Lincoln, in fact had many more computers per capita than the more affluent Longfellow. But computers did not—and I believe they cannot—make up for underlying social inequity. Neither technology nor federal and state-required testing programs will make up for that. As I left Lincoln, the final words of the Pledge rang in my ears: "with liberty and justice for all."

PART V ◄◄◄

Conclusions and Next Steps

▶▶▶ 21

Computer Use
in Our Schools

DURING MY SCHOOL VISITS, I SAW COMPUTERS USED IN FIVE different ways: as *teaching machines*, as *productivity tools*, as *Internet portals*, as *test givers*, and as *data processors*. These five categories provided me with a helpful framework for thinking about how to improve the ways that technology is used in classrooms.

Computer as Teaching Machine

When we think of computers in schools, we often think first of the computer as a teaching machine. Images pop to mind of a lab with 25 students, isolated from human interaction and peering intently at their monitors while tapping their keyboards in response to programmed prompts.

Indeed, some computer use follows this Computer-Based Training (CBT) model, but from what I observed, CBT is a small and often ineffective part of computer usage in schools. My informal survey put CBT at between 15 and 25 percent of total use, varying with grade level and curriculum area. Generally, the lower the grade level, the more the computer is used as a teaching machine. Few students in those lower grades have the skills to use it as a productivity tool: 1st graders can't type; 3rd graders can't make a spreadsheet or organize a database.

The CBT products I saw varied considerably in type and quality. They included such programs as skill-building games, intervention activities, single-user simulations, and test-prep materials. Quality ranged from little more than electronic page-turners to full-featured reading instructional support programs that engage multiple senses and support an array of print, video, and audio components.

As I note in Chapter 3, teachers often have scant interest in using CBT programs. This is ironic because, until recently, publishers have focused their resources on this type of product. Consequently, teachers find no scarcity of CBT-like materials. Special education teacher Linda Scott of Longfellow Elementary School sat at a desk covered with 50 different CD-ROM programs. In her wealthy and well-staffed district, with its small classes, she and her aides had the opportunity to become familiar with all 50 programs. Few classroom teachers can inform themselves as she does.

The teachers I visited did not relish acquiring more software; they were already burdened by a surfeit of materials and lacked the time or incentive to review and understand these materials intimately. Perhaps this surplus of material and scarcity of time explains the stagnating sales of instructional software during a period when computer usage has been rising.

I came to see that a teacher must know a program well in order to use it successfully. I came to understand that a student's sustained interest in a program depends upon the teacher's engagement. It is not a simple equation of Student + Computer = Learning, but rather Student + Computer + An Engaged Teacher = Learning. If the teacher is not engaged or does not believe that the student's activity is important, the student eventually becomes disengaged.

This presents a dilemma. Many software programs provide elaborate teacher management systems that issue valuable data on each student's performance. However, few teachers I visited had the time to digest and act upon all the data available. Think of 3rd grade teacher Belinda Short in her self-contained classroom of 25 children. She teaches language arts, mathematics, social studies, and science every day. Multiply her 25 students by the four subjects. Then assume that Belinda's students use a CBT program with each subject, and consider that each program issues data. Belinda is faced with data from 100 different student performance reports. She won't be able to use it all. Either the programs or the data will go unused.

Similarly, high school teacher Tim Higgins confronts the impossible task of evaluating performance data for the 120 students he teaches each day. In Chapter 22, I discuss a way we might address this situation: focusing computer use on students who will benefit the most from it. Although it might be unpopular, it provides a solution to a very common problem. There are too many programs and too much potential data. There is too little time.

The computer's role as teaching machine could grow in the future, but I think that growth is contingent upon significant breakthroughs in artificial intelligence, high-speed data streaming, and interface design. I suspect that the computer will evolve to a new design—possibly a tablet or handheld style—and will be only one component of a multimedia instructional program. In the meantime, the teachers and students I visited will continue to work with computers that are frequently sluggish and unengaging. I did see a few exceptions that succeeded through a rare combination of sound instructional design and high production values and committed teachers who monitored their use.

Computer as Productivity Tool

For most of us, a computer is a productivity tool. We use it to compose documents, make spreadsheets, send e-mail, create graphics, organize presentations, or build databases. Often computers make things quicker, more efficient, or easier.

That is how I saw students using computers too, especially in middle school and high school. Of course, if Johnny can't type, the computer's value as a productivity tool is significantly diminished. A few of the schools I visited had formal keyboarding instruction at the elementary grades, but in most cases, keyboarding instruction was a haphazard, hit-or-miss affair. I learned that Johnny is most likely to receive a formal keyboarding class in middle school, where he has to unlearn bad habits acquired through an uncoordinated jumble of instruction or through no instruction at all. In middle school, he also learns something about spreadsheets and presentation software, if he has not studied these earlier.

During my travels, I saw children as young as 2nd graders developing presentations with Microsoft PowerPoint. Often, students prepared these for their parents to view during open houses. PowerPoint presentations can lead students to a deep understanding of the content. Recall Mary Strickland, the veteran educator and school principal, convinced that the presentations her school's 8th graders prepared taught them much about the 1930s (see Chapter 7). More often, however, I saw student thought and energy going into exploring the mechanics of the software instead of the content being studied.

The use of computers as productivity tools represents the largest fraction of technology use in the schools. I saw the computer used as a report writer, presentation giver, digital graphics tool, and communications hub (when e-mail was available). These applications can represent 50 to 60 percent of computer usage, depending upon the grade level and academic discipline.

Computer as Internet Portal

The computer's use as Internet portal is aligned closely to its role as productivity tool. Web site images can be pasted into a report composed with a word processor. Sounds borrowed from the Web can be used in a PowerPoint presentation. The amount of Internet computer use varies by grade level and subject, but it represents approximately 20 to 30 percent of computer time in schools.

The Internet often distracts students. Teachers I visited were troubled, and not only because of concern about pornography, which is sometimes accessible despite filtering programs. Teachers were also concerned about competition from Web sites put up by ESPN, CNN, and CBS Sports, as well as myriad other pop culture sites that are not on the filter list but distract attention in the classroom. Instant messaging over the Internet is also a distraction.

The Web is like a crowded bazaar. Senses are engaged and everything is available. Pop-up ads, unsuppressed by some security programs, shout like hucksters. Where e-mail is available, spam messages intrude and make their insistent pitches. Schools try to deal with these problems with Authorized Use Policies that define acceptable access. Internet-using teachers often prequalify sites and limit their students to these approved resources. These sites become acceptable sources of information and may contain activities and images that are integral to a lesson or unit.

The advanced placement biology class at Longworth High School (see Chapter 3) modeled exceptional use of the Web. Teacher Howard Matthews prequalified a selection of Web sites and had pairs of students create their own sites, drawing from the prequalified sites. When students discovered new sites, they discussed them with Howard and learned to apply criteria for evaluating site reliability. The Internet allows Howard's students access to information that they could not have found within any school's four walls.

The Web is often less valuable at the elementary level. I frequently observed students moving helter-skelter from Web site to Web site, without the discipline to focus on the written word. Rather than digesting and summarizing the information, they cut and pasted text after a quick read. Too often, students I observed spent their time looking for graphics that moved or made sounds.

I learned that the teachers who get value from the Web have transformed it from a jumbled bazaar to an orderly shop. I saw them investing time in planning and offering careful guidance, especially to younger students. For many teachers I visited, the investment was not justified by the return.

Computer as Test Giver

Computer-based testing was used infrequently in the schools I visited, but I believe it will become a more widespread tool. High among its benefits is quick delivery of test results—just the thing, for example, for the eager students at Washington-Connors Elementary who wanted to know immediately how they performed on their practice sheets (see Chapter 4). But computers as test givers can do more than satisfy students' impatience and curiosity. They can also yield information to guide near- or long-term instruction.

Because computer-based testing allows for speedier results than pencil-and-paper tests, it is attractive for high-stakes assessment. Administrators, parents, teachers, and students all welcome faster turnaround of high-stakes results, but the computer's greatest value may lie with the assessment of daily performance. For example, Longworth High School teacher Howard Matthews already downloads test-making tools from the Internet. He develops self-correcting tests that deliver scores immediately. My visits led me to believe that a growth in prepackaged, self-scoring, computer-based tests that support textbook programs will take place in the future. In Chapter 22, I discuss more fully this emerging role of computers in delivering such assessment.

Computer as Data Processor

As I visited schools, I found that my focus slowly shifted from viewing the computer as a tool for instruction to seeing it as a data processing tool that analyzes and reports information. In the end, this may be the computer's most important role in schools. Its primary role may not be to deliver and directly support instruction, but to provide information that drives curriculum and administrative decisions. Larry Sowder, superintendent of the Washington-Connors School District (see Chapter 4), sees that potential. Larry doesn't start with a computer; he isn't even a computer user. He starts with a problem: how to decide which initiatives will have long-term effects on the lives of students. As a result, Washington-Connors is alive with exciting initiatives: Even Start; Head Start; before-school classes; after-school classes; Saturday enrichment classes; summer programs; evening instruction for parents; comprehensive computer programs for reading, math, and science; and more. Larry introduced all of these initiatives, and although it was clear to me that he believed in each, he had scant evidence of their long-range benefits.

What Larry does is look to computers for help in guiding the district's choices and investments. He asks computers to draw together all the data—family history, medical data, teacher data, report card grades, test performance, and other information, so that he can make better decisions. For example, Larry anticipated the requirements of No Child Left Behind and other federal and state legislation, which demand data-supported decisions. Now he wants computers to help align standards, instruction, and assessment in the district. In the years ahead, many superintendents and other school administrators will join Larry in doing this.

22

So What
Should We Do?

I CAME AWAY FROM MY YEAR'S WORTH OF SCHOOL VISITS WITH a mélange of observations and conclusions. Flowing from these are several recommendations, which I will expand upon later in this chapter. These are the lessons I learned from sitting in classrooms observing children and listening to teachers. Although I treated these conclusions and recommendations implicitly or explicitly in the Viewpoint sections of the previous chapters, I think it useful to summarize them here:

1. The time students spend on computers is too limited to have significant impact on measured performance.
2. The impact of computers has been diluted by the need to provide equal access to all students.
3. Computers may deliver the greatest benefit to students at the low end of the performance curve.
4. Classroom size limits successful computer use.
5. Computers can be effective tools to support alignment of standards, instruction, and assessment.

6. Schools have no shortage of software; instead, they have a surfeit of digital materials but a shortage of time to evaluate and use them.

7. Most teachers are not computer phobic, but their ability to use productivity tools does not necessarily carry over to the effective use of computers for instruction.

8. Teachers and administrators are driven by proficiency testing, which determines what is taught, how time is used, and how money is spent.

9. Technology is used best when the principal is committed and the school has a full-time technology coordinator.

10. Too much time is spent on the mechanics of computer-based tools and too little time is spent on the content being studied.

11. Computer technology is too complex to be cost-effective for many school uses.

Recommendations for Fixing the Technology Fix

"Are you doing anything different since finishing your study?"

The man almost scowled as he spoke. His question followed a talk I gave about my sabbatical. Did he disapprove of my methodology? It would not surprise me. I'd begun the study just to satisfy my own curiosity and had not intended to write a book, submit articles, or give talks. Then a field geologist friend urged me to preserve my observations. (She viewed them as data, though not quantitative data.) That is when I drafted a few sample chapters, put them in an envelope, sent them to the Association for Supervision and Curriculum Development, and eventually committed to writing this book.

I really hadn't planned on doing anything differently after my study's completion. I was simply going to go back to work and pick up where I left off a year earlier. But the man's question made me realize that I had changed, or that my view of technology had changed. Before my study, I knew computers were not a quick fix. Now I understood some reasons why they weren't and perhaps a little of what needed to be done to change things. Still, wasn't the *doing* for someone else?

Principal Jim Sneider of St. John's High School (see Chapter 6) wanted laptop computers to be the catalyst for renewal, but without his kind of leadership—without refocusing computer use from instruction to assessment and data processing, without a curriculum teaching productivity skills in a rational sequence—computers would be little more than the "boxes of wire," described by middle school teacher Rosemary Lawton (see Chapter 12). As I thought about my answer to the man's question, I realized that my journey had made me an advocate. I had winnowed from my experience a handful of recommendations that I believed in. Furthermore, I knew that I should act, however modestly, to resolve this technology fix by advocating with publishers, volunteering for my school district's technology committee, saying yes to a newspaper's request for an article on my study, talking to local university classes, and finishing this book.

My questioner's scowl, I learned in a post-talk discussion, was rooted in his insistence on an answer to the question, "So what?" My answer is found in the following recommendations. At least one recommendation may be dismissed as impractical and too politically incorrect. Another may be thought too obvious, because it is common sense to teach productivity tools at the right time and in sequence. If that is so obvious, though, why is it done with such infrequency? I have boiled my recommendations down to four.

Recommendation #1: *Focus computer use on students who will benefit most; don't dilute the value of computers by insisting that all students have equal access.* Teachers make choices every day. As curriculums tighten under the influence of the standards movement, teacher choice has been restricted. A teacher might not be allowed to teach her butterfly unit again this year if it does not align with science, social studies, or language arts standards.

Schools need to make choices about how they will use computer time. Often these choices are left to teachers. Understanding administrators will have trouble telling teachers that certain students will use computers and certain students won't. To do so goes against time-honored traditions of teacher choice and educational commitment to equal treatment of all students.

However, lots of time-honored traditions are changing. Most obvious is that schools today do provide special treatment for students with learning, physical, or behavioral disabilities. Their special needs—and the special needs of gifted students, second language learners, and other specific populations—are accounted for when school services are parceled out. Simply put, because their needs are greater, they get more of the education dollar than students in the middle do.

Should special-needs or challenged learners get more computer time, too? I believe they should. A choice must be made: Either every student spends an hour a week at a computer, with little gain, or computer use can focus on those who will benefit most.

"Those are not the only alternatives," someone might object. "Simply use all the time available and every student can use a computer four or five hours a week."

It is not so simple. That solution overlooks the management problem at the root of computer under-use. Keeping every computer in constant use demands time and managerial finesse that teachers don't have. There is more to effective computer use than sitting students in front of a computer: The teacher must select programs that support the curriculum, that align to achievement levels, and that the teacher knows thoroughly. The teacher needs time to analyze where each student is now and where he or she is going next. A teacher can't do that for 25 computer-using students and teach simultaneously.

My previous sentence betrays a view of teaching that conflicts with technological pundits' view of the teacher as a facilitator of student learning. Teachers are repeatedly urged to abandon their role as "sage on the stage" and reposition themselves as a "guide on the side." The fact is that with the addition of technology to the classroom, they need to be the "sage on the side," guiding students in the use of computers and other instructional materials while retaining their role as content authorities. There is not an intrinsic conflict between the teacher-driven, content-centered curriculum and the child-centered curriculum; but there is a conflict between the time available and the demands on that time.

Until there are simpler technologies and quantum leaps in the application of artificial intelligence so that every student has immediate access at all times to electronic tools, choices will have to be made. For pedagogical and pragmatic reasons, I believe those choices should favor students at the low end of the performance curve. The pedagogical basis is that low-performing students benefit more from the orderliness of computer-based instruction. Better-performing students often possess the organizational skills that struggling students lack. For struggling students, the computer helps supply the order that they need. If one accepts that a computer is patient, as Principal Peter Malone pointed out in Chapter 2, computers would seem to possess an important virtue for helping low-performing students.

Of course, this assumes that the "patient" computer's software is well designed and engaging. Even quality software will not sustain engagement without teacher support. Dull, poorly designed, unimaginative software cannot be redeemed, whatever the teacher's engagement.

The pragmatic basis for focusing on struggling students relates to test scores. Students at the low end of the performance curve have a disproportionately negative effect on classroom, school, and district averages. Bring those scores up through attentive use of instructional software and we will see disproportionately positive gains.

Some will object, saying that we should focus instead on students just below the passing level. Providing a small boost to these students is thought easier than giving a substantial boost to students at the low end of the performance curve. This pragmatic talk may be unsettling, but it is realistic in today's environment. The problem with elevating the performance of students who stand on the threshold of success is that the main burden falls on the classroom teacher. There are more efficient ways, as I discuss in my next recommendation, for raising the performance level of students in the middle, including those on the brink of passing.

If you accept that successful computer use depends upon the active support of a teacher, there is a greater chance that support will be available for the lower-performing student. It is impractical to send a student to a computer and expect substantial gains without any teacher involvement. Focus on a few students—with the help of a specialist, a resource teacher, or an aide, if available—and success becomes possible. Current funding programs make these specialists available to support lower-performing students with special needs.

The public relations challenge of this approach cannot be minimized. Parents want their children to use computers; they believe computers are essential to current learning and future success. But we know that computer use has led to minimal measurable performance gain to date and that computers of the future will be radically different from those in schools today. The computer parade will not pass by the 2nd grader who is not taught PowerPoint. Schools need to make choices, believe in those choices, and explain those choices.

Focusing on the needs of the few does not mean ignoring the opportunities for the many. A well designed, developmentally appropriate computer curriculum can help ensure that all students acquire skills when they need them. It does not have to be rushed, but it has to be right, as I discuss in my third recommendation.

Recommendation #2: *Use computers to support the alignment of standards, instruction, and assessment.* My first recommendation deals with lower-performing students. This second recommendation can benefit all students, especially the bulk of students who fall in the broad middle range of student performance.

For students in the middle, the computer can support learning and increase test scores by helping to align standards, instruction, and assessment. It can do this more efficiently than it can deliver instruction for large numbers of students.

High-stakes tests and classroom teaching have often been misaligned. If the tests contain material that has not been taught, too much is left to chance—and chances are that students will lose out.

I am not recommending teaching to the test or relying on test-prep programs. If standards, instruction, and assessment are aligned, teachers can teach to the curriculum and feel assured that students will be test-ready. The challenge lies in developing and executing an aligned curriculum.

Here, the computer can help. There are a number of information management systems available to school administrators today. The best of these provide blueprints and tools for aligning curriculum. Still, computer programs don't do the work; it is an analytic tool, not a panacea. Alignment is the work of administrators and teachers, and it's hard work, even with these tools. It requires the commitment of teams who understand their district's curriculum, the instructional materials used in the district, and the characteristics of their district's assessment programs.

I recall sitting in a room on a sweltering August day with 33 teachers from 9 districts as they struggled with aligning standards, instruction, and assessment of their writing strands. The districts belonged to a countywide consortium that was committed to curricular alignment. The teachers had to learn the language and procedures of a complex new software program; they had to draw upon their individual and collective knowledge of writing instruction; and they had to understand the assessment style that their state and district tests used. Why? Starting in the fall, they would be part of a pilot program to improve writing achievement in the nine districts. Writing had been identified as the Achilles heel of the language arts curriculum. Test score analysis had shown that writing test scores pulled down measured performance levels.

The districts' solution was not to set a vague goal to use computers to teach each student to write better. The solution was to use computers to ensure that what was tested had been taught, whatever the method or materials used. Additionally, the teachers identified indicators of success or failure and began the challenging task of building a repository of lesson plans and resources that have proved successful in teaching each writing skill.

Curriculum alignment is not only difficult, it can be disruptive. A teacher must ensure that her yearly butterfly unit aligns with the district's science, social studies, or reading standards—and that means that there may be fewer butterfly units in the future. Textbooks must be scoured to ensure that they cover the content to be tested at year's end. Publishers usually provide correlation guides that show how their programs' content supports the state or district curriculum.

A powerful computer program can digest this and other information, allowing the teacher to access a standard and see what material addresses it, what material can be used with students who require remediation, and what type of formal or informal assessments can be used to ensure that the standard has been met. A computer program can help a teacher keep track of which standards have been covered and how students have performed on the assessments related to them.

Despite the hard work, I am convinced that this is an extremely efficient use of computer power. Curriculum alignment is essential, and the computer can be an essential tool in achieving it.

Recommendation #3: *Use computers for assessment; benefit from their ability to correct tests automatically and provide results quickly.* "The children love to use the scanners," Gloria Hauser, a 3rd grade teacher at Washington-Connors Elementary School told me (see Chapter 4). Initially, I was puzzled by this. A scanner is a pretty ordinary device. The students insert an answer card in front and it pops out the back. On the surface, it seems no big deal. But what pops up on the computer screen *is* a big deal: Students get near-instant results.

Immediate feedback to the students is an important benefit of computer-based testing, but it's not the only one. Automatic scoring saves significant time for teachers. Test-scoring tools are available for judging constructed response and essay questions as well. Although recently introduced, they are growing in sophistication and power. Test scoring is an area where many teachers do not mind being replaced.

As this is written, 13 U.S. states are experimenting with computer-delivered high-stakes tests. Eight more states have plans to begin such a program. The numbers will grow as a variety of practical issues are resolved. These issues are significant now, making the near-term use of the computer on a widespread basis for high-stakes tests impractical. Test publishers and districts are still struggling with technological, administrative, and psychometric issues. Technology issues include the instability of school networks; the variety of hardware, network speeds, and bandwidth; and security issues. Administrative issues include schedule conflicts between testing and instructional use of computers and the need to ensure that students who are tested last do not have an advantage over students who are tested earlier. For example, if limited access to computers results in a three-week testing period, will students who are tested at the end of that period be exposed to more content than students tested at the beginning?

Psychometric issues include comparability between print versions and computer versions of a test, whether students with a considerable amount of computer experience have an advantage over students with little, and whether personality type influences how students perform on computer-based versus printed tests. On printed tests, some students skip questions and then go back. Computer-based tests do not usually provide this option. Psychometrists wonder if computer tests penalize students who are accustomed to skipping and going back.

Issues like these are more important for high-stakes tests than for regular classroom tests. They will be solved in time. Networks will be stabilized and strengthened; computer specifications will become more uniform; security and administrative concerns will be resolved. That is because the payoff can be so high. Because high-stakes testing is a political as well as an educational issue, there is strong pressure to produce accurate results quickly. Federal and state legislation offers rewards and imposes penalties based upon test results. Spring tests have serious implications for fall placement of students. Poor school performance can entitle students to change schools or qualify them for supplemental services. Strong performance can result in supplemental pay for teachers and administrators or enhanced revenue for their schools. The public—and real estate agents—wait anxiously for publication of school rankings. All of these pressures will stimulate the search for solutions to the current barriers to widespread computer-based high-stakes testing.

The economic slowdown of the early 21st century will also slow the move to computer-based testing. It costs more at the beginning to adapt or create computer tests and put in place the required technological and administrative systems. In an era of tight budgets, deferrable expenses get deferred. But it will happen, and the groundwork for change is being laid. The kids in Gloria Hauser's class, and others I saw like them, are a microcosm of the public's enthusiasm for quick test results. We are an impatient people accustomed to instant cash, instant food, and instant communication through cell phones.

Demand for near-immediate test results will drive the solution to the problems that slow down computerized high-stakes testing. Already, certification and licensure tests in many medical and business specialties are delivered by computer. The lessons learned there will be carried over to high-stakes testing in schools.

Many certification and licensure tests use what is called a Computer Adaptive Test (CAT). A CAT uses a different statistical model for test item analysis. It is more complex than that used in traditional test norming. On a CAT, the computer presents test items based upon the test taker's previous answers. If the test taker does well on questions, he or she is propelled forward to more difficult items. The result is a shorter test period. CATs are far more efficient than standard tests, though more costly to develop. They are widely used in business and licensure exams because they save valuable time for administrators and test takers. Although federal officials responsible for enforcing provisions of the No Child Left Behind legislation have ruled that CATs do not meet the letter of the law, CATs are likely to become a standard for school testing in the future. With time so valuable to teachers, I believe CATs will be readily embraced.

While the issues for high-stakes testing are being resolved, computer use for formal, low-stakes testing will take root and grow in the classroom. This is the low-stakes assessment that is intrinsic to a course while it is being studied—lesson, chapter, or unit tests.

These tests are not subject to the same rigors as high-stakes testing, but the attraction of immediate results and the advantages of automatic correcting still apply.

Beyond the value of producing immediate results, computerized low-stakes tests have the ability to direct students back to material they need to study further and to propel them forward, past material they have mastered to material that challenges. If the course content aligns to standards and the tests are carefully constructed, results can predict a student's score on a high-stakes test covering the same content area.

A somewhat similar type of assessment, called Curriculum Based Measurement (CBM), also lends itself to computer administration. Unlike conventional assessments, which usually focus on the mastery of content that has just been taught, a CBM test covers all relevant content for a semester or year. CBM tests are administered periodically and yield measures of growth. This growth can be graphed for individual students or classes and can guide teachers in adjusting instruction or modifying the curriculum.

I recommend that schools focus computer use on assessment. In the near-term, this can mean conventional mastery assessments or CBM-type tests. Meanwhile, the electronic infrastructures should be strengthened to accommodate the security, speed, and bandwidth required for high-stakes tests. The payback will come from enhanced performance in the classroom and rapid delivery of high-stakes test results.

Recommendation #4: *Teach students to use productivity tools and the Internet, but wait until students are ready; coordinate such teaching within and across grade levels.* Penmanship was once a prized craft. Every student was taught a handwriting method. At the border of the chalkboard were sample alphabets to be studied and emulated. And it was an important day when one transitioned to stick pen, metal point, and black ink.

Those days are but a memory for a few of us. In that long-ago time, there was careful articulation between the pencil-and-printing of the early grades and the cursive pen writing that came later. In this technological era, that sequencing of skills is often lost. Some states and districts have standards for computer skill development. Some have guidelines for teaching Internet use. From my observation, this was left to the classroom teacher and sometimes the lab director to implement. In an hour a week, little skill development was accomplished at the elementary grades unless there was a tightly structured keyboarding program like that at St. Mary's Elementary School (see Chapter 1). Otherwise, it was hit or miss until middle school, where keyboarding was usually taught.

In my school visits, I saw only rudimentary instruction in Internet use. Students received some familiarization with Internet browsers and search methods but this, too, was often unstructured and left to the personal whim of the classroom teacher or lab director. Students sometimes taught one another, which had its positive aspects.

In some of the more technologically advanced schools, I sensed a rush to teach productivity tools. Second and 3rd graders were taught PowerPoint basics. Fourth graders used digital cameras for science reports or personal biographies. Fifth graders made spreadsheets. The focus of these exercises was usually on features and functions of the software, not on the content. They were usually not part of a developmentally appropriate curriculum.

Standards exist, but teachers at the classroom level are seldom aware of them. The International Society for Technology in Education (ISTE) has published a set of curriculum and content standards for grades K–12. ISTE's National Educational Technology Standards (available at http://www.iste.org/standards/) have been adopted, adapted, or referenced in the curriculum documents of 44 states. They have influenced written policies, but have not been translated into an orderly sequence of instruction in many schools.

The standards are comprehensive and sequential, but I believe they call for too much too soon. For example, a standard for kindergarten through grade 2 reads: "Create developmentally appropriate multimedia products with support from teachers, family members, or student partners." What is "developmentally appropriate" in this context? Is it PowerPoint for kindergarteners, and if so, for what purpose?

I don't wish to nitpick. The ISTE standards have been assembled by experienced technology leaders. They represent an advocacy position that is understandable. I believe, however, that skills recommended for the early grades can be pushed to later grades without loss to anyone. Tools will change. Computers will become smaller, faster, and more intuitive. The 2nd graders who do not learn to create a PowerPoint presentation will not be at a disadvantage in tomorrow's employment marketplace. They will be if they are unable to read.

What I saw was a huge gap between ISTE recommendations and reality. ISTE standards call for students to type by the end of grade 5, yet in many systems, typing is a staple of the middle school curriculum. There are administrative and financial reasons for this. The middle school schedule, with its specialized classes, lends itself to making typing classes available to students. It is harder to arrange for an experienced instructor and a dedicated class period at the elementary school level. Consequently, keyboarding instruction is left for the teacher to implement, and most teachers decide against taking the time. To meet the ISTE keyboarding standard, elementary schools would need significantly different class schedules and staffing models.

In one middle school I visited, keyboarding instruction represented the bulk of lab usage. Keyboarding was a yearlong course for every student, whether or not they came to class with keyboarding skills. These extensive classes absorbed virtually all of the middle school lab time; if teachers wanted to use computers for something other than keyboard instruction, they had to use their classroom computers. Why was keyboarding instruction such a priority? The funding to hire the lab teacher came from a vocational education grant. The instructors were trained vocational education teachers who wanted each student to be prepared for an administrative position in business. This may have been overkill, with the financial tail wagging the curriculum dog.

As I noted earlier, this may seem an obvious recommendation, but computer skills instruction needs to be rethought. If computer use is refocused on the students who need it most and on assessment, there will be less time for skills instruction. That instruction has its purpose, but it may take place later than ISTE recommends without loss to students. Later instruction will bring quicker learning on the newer tools that students will encounter in the workplace.

ISTE has also issued comprehensive standards for preservice teacher training, with special emphasis on student teaching and the new teacher's first year in the classroom. The influence of these is evident in the course offerings of teacher training programs. Some states and districts are slowly establishing requirements for inservice training as well.

I've said little about training in this book, but that's not because it is unimportant. It is quite necessary, but it is simply not sufficient. The larger issues of purpose, alignment, and focus have to be settled for teacher training to pay off. If the focus of technology in schools is not corrected, technology courses will not be able to accomplish what is needed.

▶ ▶ ▶

Will my four recommendations remove the scowl from my questioner's face? Or will they merely deepen it? "So what?" he challenged me. In these recommendations, I tried to answer that challenge. I want to see our schools get out of the technology fix so many of them are in. I want to see technology's potential realized and its promise fulfilled. It is a promise that can be kept.

Acknowledgments ◄◄◄

MANY PEOPLE MADE THIS BOOK POSSIBLE. MOST IMPORTANT were the administrators and teachers who invited me into their schools and classrooms. This close-up look would not have been possible without their help and interest. Thanks to my editor John DeSimon for his wise guidance as I shaped the manuscript; to Ellen Dawson-Witt, who read the manuscript and nagged me about details of grammar and style; and to Martha Hild, who encouraged me to translate my field notes into a book. I owe special thanks to Bill Franklin, president of the Mazer Corporation, who generously allowed me to spend a year on this study; and to my colleagues, who covered for me while I was gone and endured obsessive descriptions of what I had seen when I returned. And finally, thanks to my wife, Helen, who not only offered constant encouragement but also graciously put up with my fretting and overlooked that the house is a year overdue for painting.

Index ◄◄◄

Note: Pseudonymous names are not specially marked. See author note concerning names in the text.

About the Author ◄◄◄

WILLIAM D. PFLAUM'S OLDEST SON WENT OFF TO COLLEGE lugging an Osborne computer. The Osborne, the earliest commercial portable computer, weighed 20 pounds and had a 3-inch screen. Back then, Bill believed in the promise of computers for his family, himself, his business, and schools. He still does.

Bill is a graduate of the University of Notre Dame with a degree in English. After serving in the military in the early 1960s, he earned a master's degree in education from the Catholic University of America. Since then, he has written, edited, and managed the development of a wide range of print and digital materials for the classroom. He has been president of a parochial school board and founding board president of a school for children with serious learning disabilities. He currently serves on the board of a regional science museum. He can be reached at wdpflaum@ix.netcom.com.

Related ASCD Resources for Technology in Schools

At the time of publication, the following ASCD resources were available. ASCD stock numbers are noted in parentheses.

Audiotapes
Critical Components of Effective Technology Training by Larry E. Lindon (#297050)
Redesigning and Reevaluating Your School's Technology Plan by Vicki Barnett, Mary Jane Simmons, and Kim Sukackson (#201148)
Using Technology Raises Student Test Scores by Ted Ammann and Susan Giancola (#201122)

Multimedia
Project-Based Learning with Multimedia CD-ROM by the San Manteo County Office of Education (1 hybrid CD-ROM) (#502117)
The Research on Technology for Learning CD-ROM by North Central Regional Educational Laboratory (1 hybrid CD-ROM) (#597001)

Online Resources
Visit the ASCD Web Site (http://www.ascd.org) to search current and archived articles from *Curriculum/Technology Quarterly*, the ASCD newsletter exploring how educators in the classroom use technology to improve teaching and learning. Also, click on "Professional Development" to find out more about ASCD Professional Development Online Courses such as "Planning for Technology" and "Teaching Better with Technology."

Networks
Visit the ASCD Web site (http://www.ascd.org) and search for "networks" for information about professional educators who have formed groups around topics like "Integrating Technology in the Elementary Classroom" and "Technology in the Middle School." Look in the "Network Directory" for current facilitators' contact information.

Print Products
Educational Leadership: Teaching Better with Technology (Vol. 56, No. 5, February 1999) (#199026)
Increasing Student Learning Through Multimedia Projects by Michael Simkins, Karen Cole, Fern Tavalin, and Barbara Means (#102112)
The Internet and the Law: What Teachers Need to Know by Kathleen Conn (#102119)
The New Basics: Education and the Future of Work in the Telematic Age by David Thornburg (#102005)
Teaching Every Student in the Digital Age: Universal Design for Learning by David H. Rose and Anne Meyer (#101042)
Visual Literacy: Learn to See, See to Learn by Lynell Burmark (#101226)

For additional resources, visit us on the World Wide Web (http://www.ascd.org), send an e-mail message to member@ascd.org, call the ASCD Service Center (1-800-933-ASCD or 703-578-9600, then press 2), send a fax to 703-575-5400, or write to Information Services, ASCD, 1703 N. Beauregard St., Alexandria, VA 22311-1714 USA.